AF378928

Morpheu

A.M.J. Crawford

BlazeVOX [books]

Buffalo, New York

Morpheu by A.M.J. Crawford
Copyright © 2009

Published by BlazeVOX [books]

All rights reserved. No part of this book may be reproduced without
the publisher's written permission, except for brief quotations in reviews.

The author would like to thank the US Fulbright Commission, the Portuguese
Fulbright Commission, & the Instituto Camões for sponsoring this project.

Printed in the United States of America

Book design by Geoffrey Gatza

First Edition

ISBN 13: 9781935402060
Library of Congress Control Number: 2008943133

BlazeVOX [books]
14 Tremaine Ave
Kenmore, NY 14217

Editor@blazevox.org

publisher of weird little books

BlazeVOX [books]

blazevox.org

2   4   6   8   0   9   7   5   3   1

B   X

Morpheu

Say quite by chance there's one sees these ineptitudes
my readers to be and with such hands as might
touch never horrified to move toward us

–Louis Zukofsky

†ARGUMENTUM†

mission briefing.
    how vague?
omicron vague.
    omg.

        well is it homotopic?

     container,
  yr eyes we have sheep-
       dipped/
           in a cool-
        salty wash,

    we call you an agglutination,
     we call you Pierrot,

       the mariner, the back-
  engineer of the boat—

      the boat?

         container,
          the craft/
           the ship,
      the SS Nantucket to be clear,

we sail?

   //dilating time//

     Do you know of the island of stability?
  I do.
     Good.
      Here.

Have a complimentary letter opener†

    bon voyage

I

Traces of Gold

TACITURN with lips that murmur what confederate winds press back,
and heavy breath that whangs/

            there is gold inlaid in me†

        encrusted with rare stones,

      ominous gold,
        the very clank of medieval bronze†

        What is precious though

    is faceted in a makedo varnish/

     that is Initial.

      and will bleed another instance.

That makes for a slow start,

           though the Soul will twerk

    its Tender/

     lathering itself

  in a salve of scalar radiation/

        whereby the nearest glyph will slalom

       mole 2 mole

      //down//

      Down the nape of its own neck

     "as does the beading sweat/the sun cajoles

    along the rim of its smug meniscus,"

      paring its thinning blood

        by the mettle of its Smooth

   Pursuit,

     feeding off the tallow of a warm-rich saccade

Chiefing its bling/

       a hotboxed whole-grain Ciborium.

What is a true caucus of Loss

is holding its writ by the Node

of its wizened proxy//snuffing its trysts//

"yr mourning yr quiet
hooves,"

"yr pigeon-
toed para-
diddle-
diddle
para-
diddle-
diddle

FLAM!

Ratamacue,
and then the bass dropped

beneath yr capsid,

"in the hull of yr chiral center,"

said
Pierrot.

Pierrot
liked sucking on a pecan log from time 2 time;

Pierrot
liked the poop deck for the view,
"I remember, *prick*!"

//phase shift//

"once there was a princess
the word stuck
trust me."

my trill aphasia/

"yr leafed and lamel-
     lar cask/

                    ...like those helmets
               Moloch's team's
                    got/

               their catalyzed
          platinum ping

                    in the tortoise shell style"

     //glottal stomp//

          there was a clown
     it rapped its monocle
          to clear an atavistic throat,
                    a vessel in-
                         deed...

                    end quote.

     En-
       gine
     jar-
       gon.
               Report 1.
"this is not what really happened."

                    "Jim Barns my friend, dictation!"

"first. on the subject of its queer mast/I negate
     not the vertical, but any semblance of a-
bove."

               ...dreaming of a blue tail-
                    fly/

                         "I lick the sex-
                    tant at the tip;
                         I am thinking

                    I am ex-
                         punging
                    yr herald complex" he wrote,

transfusing yr oxytocin wings in-
to an oxycotton fang,

end quote.

advisory. flapjack murder on the level of its calyx/

a curdled alpha *eleven, twenty, twenty-
one, twenty-two, thirty-nine*

...the captain loved suspense...he had a great sense
of humor...and so he paused for three days
before announcing
the number on
the Power Ball
//littoral silence//

no one even shat
then suddenly...you could hear a pin-
ball drop
beneath her
speakers'
trypsin
crackle...

machine gun fire! No.

"just a crew re-
capping its pens."

Deject yourself Pierrot,
no one ever seems to win.

"mark. this map it
smells
of a cheap fiber-
optic brocade,"

"a rich powder, yes
trust me,"

                              "yr registered
                                 smile,"

                    I was deepthroating yr cig
                       long before yr gummy
                    freaknik/

                       "yr shrapnel was a heavy lacquered wood
                    on who's chest?"

               I am now up-
          loading
                    a memory
            of that time in-
          side
                    the manufacturing hall.

       months ago.
the day you gave me the job.

          Buffering...

                         "this ship is bigger
                              than yr mega-
          church."
                              "yes. even if you count the north
          campus."

                         "its dubious double-
                              glazing Jim their liars!"

          "were floating on a trophy of the fall."

          "and then he turned said yeah sure
          and my hand is cut jasper,"

                    no seriously touch it.

          "possibly the strangest feature
               was the bridge
          see the draw
bridge to the bridge
               wore an oxy-
                    dized
                         coat"

&so

    its lower jaw

its plugged nostrils

  &intense
inter-
personal attraction(mind you)
            wouldn't just
           wouldn't budge.

     Apropos opium.

      "at what level
    do you rate yr fear
      of bacteria?"

        "I have a window-
     seat voucher,"

           "as well as
         a well-
          bred path-
        ogenic coy

          smirk."

         "really?"

    "cross my prosthesis..."

      //Traces of Fake//

   Pierrot building fire
     on the beach

//oppressor complex//
                   citizen Clang.
    "yr kitsch outweighs
      yr anti-
   body count,"

       "for one/you breathe

              like you're the day-

              lily in the womb of
              my wunderkind,"

        "a smoldering industrial
      rug-factory,
            yes,
    she wore a pensive
     anxious incandescence."

I crack 'd the egg o 'er a large hot-
     Lodestone.

        "Sitting round a circle of worn divans
           they were

          Isomerizing their intent
        in a quarterly re-
            port."

              The sweet swart sweat
              of their sails goes

                   Pang.

             "Crowns onto a wet floor."

        ...&when they kindled their splints together,

            the crew intoned,

        "We Want Change"

&a neurotrophic factor-calculator
pirated itself//ergo//it began
to calculate change to n digits.

"the tide isn"t low enough"

      we sel et er
   s lo é/

         di
  des tis

(light in light)

of un-
rest/

"You illuminate a very
punctuated fear of torpor"

Dear Halogen,

          In what spectrum
did you cast

    the light of yr ghost?

 *in the weeks
following their divorce,*

        the moon became the soul,

unseen, signed Salomé.

            "squeeze a little
on yr titties
                4 me baby."

Good girl.

"let the fat bounce,"

Good.

    "I
   was
  thinking
 of milk,"

nugatory. no milf/

      Let's touch on theory
    later,

        Lest the song beest
        the key
          to me/

sticking it.”

“&of its tender synthesis?” he tongued

“STOP. save your breath for the blowjob,”

“yr luscious fever

blistered lips,”

“yr pin-
prick fluid
   drain,”

“you are gumming me, good”

Barns!
a minor note!

castrato
“For no matter the structures of dance/
   courtship never changes its denominator,

just prudence.”

I just came inside my lacuna,

end quote.

“What uncomfortable cold,
is drying here?”

“What humanizing purpure,”

“Did you say something, Herod?”

“Yes, bring me a napkin & the head of John the Baptist.”

“Would you have them, on plates of silver?”

“The napkin, yes”

//nocturnal dross//

there was a stress-cracked

Cauldron Convo.

&then a Sterile Dark
        first-
        draft;
                "Rebuke it in-
        2 this paper sac,
                Pierrot,"

        "You're jus seasick,"

    "though yr
machinations

    were an angel-
dust of H$_2$0,"

            "Arguably,"

            "Arguably,"

        "you were an inundation
            of yr own
        amarant/sibilant/
                credo-
                balk."

"advance, Islander,
    hydrogenate yr flame,"

        "your dreams
    are not your visions'

even hypotheticals"

        //roe-gossip//

septic
    assonance dis-
        association/

        "catalyze my false remembrance please!

my meat hurts."

"your chicory vesper
        was a certain
                ivory
                    vamp
                        smoke!"

"yr sound particles

they were like an army
            of white/

"I only mean they winnowed out their ribbons."

            "stop touching it, Pierrot,

            //Antiphon//

            micaceous drone,

                    "Your index was
                a lowball
                            light-flog,
                                    <u>BARNS!!</u>"

    I chronicled her vibes, er-
    go/*digital audio extraction*;

"your emissaries were
a blinding drum and
bugle corps,"

        //tornado drill//

        a fade away

    BRICK

advisory. primer heightens risk of
                lightning strikes,

                    Scheiße/
            sha-
        clack,

    Scheiße/

It is carrying the arms
            of a certain
chiasmus,"

It is settled then.

        I make a break
@low-tide,

"for the moon he
    is growing
    more feint,"

        //Agitator//

            a smelling
            salt-substitution/

                "yes. we are rationing
                our stock."

        Operation
Tamarind Switch is in effect until 7:00 p.m.

            "yr shock-
            waft graft gave
                    me a bronchial
            condition,"

    "there was a certain slip-
page to yr petty coma
        toke"

        "its plexiglas shadow,
            yes"

            "there was a bomb in the chapel
                of yr canon!"

We advise that you please clear the area,
        good day.

    & then...

"what giant mounds
of scented wax,"

tarp all of it!

"see if she starts breathing again."

my sign reads Drip-Tube Decantation,

"so much decantated and
a horizontal autocracy to be clear/

You voted in our filters,"

"you trickle out/onto the floors of altars and Whole-

Sale Gel
Candles,"

"yr talk is of the urn/

as if it were a receptacle tester,"

"I am plugging in yr filed-down mountain-
top siding,"

"wait. let it chafe

like the inside
of the inside
of an intransferable
grey quotient,"

"no! not into the trash cache."

& so again we tore the mast down.

and then the engine flooded.

and the GPS stopped working.

And when the air conditioning died/

we were left un-
comfortable

//By & by//

"I strayed into a desert,"

"mark! ~~treading
moonlight ash~~,"

moribund/

I am once again met
by my Common origin,

a morphological nightmare/

inflorescence†

"yr whistling <u>BRACT</u>
o' er a deep pocket of water"

~~this is where the tufted sand
didst render
cosmic fronds~~

yr acid green,

"what cool airs,"

~~an air de cour~~†

"yr bomb serum was our chief
antagonist,"

ergo,
a deviant lunar induction,
&so...

"yr glint is un-
like the chine

of this dithering
blade,"

"a psychotropic dust,"

yes.

"it was always just the frogs & yr detritus,"

    "it appears
they vomit u back/

        They are irritated by a fine mist of lye

            It settled to the ground,

                Tough on grease

    //fade out//

entry dating three weeks prior.

            the ship
            was alw-
            ays gon-
            na sink.

            "there is
              a basin
            in the
            bottom of my right eye."

        stick a needle in it†

        "you stagger,

            implying yr
            purpose fro-
        m the back o-
            f the neck of
            a brown pa-
              stel,

        "crack it!"

        peeling ba-
          ck the trac-
            es of a veg-
          as gold,

            yr mud ma-

sk has a fr-
othed core,

there
was
a film wai-
ting its tu-
rn to ex-
pose itself,
"~~o? do my panty~~
~~lines upset u?~~"

//surface tension//

"I am not speaking
of some car-
cinogenic

Atomic Umber,"

but of an instant hand
sanitizer abortion in-
jection.

"To leaf away/u will lodge
yrself in a glycerin
grove,"

hum. shredding
the ballistics report
he stagnated forth/

drudging his dread))
1.
"they removed
their balsa felt-
lined plank from
its maple casing;

un-
folding its velve-
teen frock
they clamped it on
2
the

hip

of the SS Nantucket
    to be clear,
                        "he walks
            today"
        two.

    the idea

is that it snaps
                before the drama
really has its chance
    to play
        out."

                    C,

"ker p
  -lunk/
                    ceremony's over."

hum. ~~no memory but~~
~~the monocle~~/

tethered
    to an ax-
    on root,
                //RIP//

        hum.
    my left temporal
        lobe is sore/

                        it stays, ~~hum~~

I judge this light as always on

            brown-
        out,

    "ready for
        yr wick

        to interrupt"

...terra firma,

she queefed.

a
dim
bog
in-
d
 e
 e
d

yr border
line/hair

line/rip-
arian zone pave-

over hold up!

"is that
a red
coat
 shank

or waht?"

"cried the oculist,"

via some wire-
 less epistolary
  miracle
   pill,

"yr rust
 it has tu-
 rned 2
lichen,"

Yes,

"emaciate yr-

                             self,”
            down
                 grade

            //STOP//

            frenetic
         phonetic/stop.

doctor/

                 .

      ..prescribing

an iso-

         pro-

            pyl

pressure-

            wash

         de-
      tox STAT/
                 No_Retort.

         “I’m not yr in-
      sulating non-

conductive catalog
   aluminum ladder,”
                        “is there a plugin
                           I can pirate 4 that?”

                     “u_c,
we don’t have
any health insurance,”

                              “They don’t have any health in-
                              surance!”
                                 “diet-food carnivore!”

"You aint nothin but a tupperware schizo,"

(walk this tightrope ——————————————————————)

There was a distance

        "yes.
the kind that proffers
        flowers."
                        hum. *She* was a writhen hollow
                                water-
                                        front

        //Advisory//

        Galleon never made bay,
                Cargo lost, stop.

we were carrying
        her corpse,
        stop.

                "Princess,

                we post-
        poned the annual

                        moonlight regatta
                        for two business days
                        in your honor,"

        we possess a latex
        neon violet,

                "what an animant
        sackful of morning glory seeds;"

"this is not an Inland Spadix,
        Sable Soil."

        "so blanch me more
                than a carmine redaction"
yes!
        To skin a golden shadow†

I pared its purple
 membrane
                from the bottom of our sweat
                        shop gum
                        stuck
                        soles,
                        there†

            triple-
                bogey

                    //Apotheosis//

            I am an anxious catalytic sponge
                    4U.

II

The Oak Cabinet

Even dead souls can signify; twice-vanished, they linger, musk, me-

                                    me.   tide   un-
                              tied.
                        double.

            back.   double.

         negative.   blacker.

            hollower.   more.

            hallow.   more.

      stranger.   good.
                                bye.   stranger.

            good.   bye.

                              chimera/

                  I am no ghost but a transparency.

            call me pallid.
                  paned.

I was last to abandon ship.

   "The ship was made of glass."

The glass was not broken/

      it was the sea that was draining.

         "my white
palms my wet
            palms,"

"my tear
      ducts
   trigger

massive sweats,"

"yr waters use-
    less,"

"what we have
      here

   is no plunger,"

              text 050808
                   to vote-
                      in our
                        vortex,

       it was viewer response that really crack' d our bow,

yr derelict body-
   trip and pyro-
plastic freestyle
   saved u,

       a stabling deposition, yes

              a convalescent garden

shade, perhaps yr ears are burning

              //jinx//

              ultraviolet over
              load at dusk
                      sharp†

                   it made it,

   "it was meant to,"
                   "thats b=a=n=a=n=a=s,

       that sandalwood jus spoke!"

"yr shadows glow like myth does,"

       "you have/what they call/a magnetical intestinal
       tract,"

       advisory. that very frond has a fake mouth,

"ventilator ventriloquism,"

yr gossamer condensation was dialectical holy water,

                                   "hs   f   o
                  g   s

                  e
                  t   u   pn mrk n
                    t e
                  e   of   t   ht
                  s
                  ma   t c in g   !"

"what heavy gumption!"

                     "in a tower somewhere
                       they laid
                     a cardboard Salomé
                        to rest
                     on a catafalque,"

                     three teenage
                       girls kept **V**igil™

                                      h
                     aving won a raffle,

                     "I lined their pads in a
                     vintage
                       raw veal,"

             "
n ,
   ces h   jr v
owz, kn
t   r
    j   ec vtttan k
   o,,
s."

"today, a make-do pestle, tomorow"

"how venerable."

and when it was
whispered it was re-
mastered/

naturally, it was first
produced by the sun/

it was called
upon

like the anthem of a war

plus ginseng,

"yr stem & spline
has not been re-
set,"

they liken yr soft
soft snaps,

"we should of jammed their cells
we jammed their banks instead."

that's no lye
that's MSG,

mmmmmmoloch,

~~"yr flint keys iz janglin
g my powder
keg,"~~

~~ergo/~~I named the moon as my prime-
minister

cause he says he'll switch

our locomotor
feeding habits,

Promising every-
Body a capital atlatl,

&a mailin rebate 4 the scope.

I developed an organic ataxia/

we are mainlining my crosshairs instead / c

u flake like the skin off a dead soul,

yr horizon was a wayward lantern/

"so imprecate me!"

"I was an amniotic satin phoenix,"

"I was marginalized for having a
sweet tooth,"

"I was razed that way,"

"I seem to be fishing for a certain
ivory tusk in the mud,"

"I cant read this effing
mimeo."

careful, Pierrot,

u just preened yr widow tax†

"another gray day," he sighed

//champagne tap//

"yr bitterness was expensive perfume"

smelt like elegant sulfur†

"what
luxury,

the last rose,
in thc last vase,"

"whose stalk is bare,

shall see you
as a fountain.”

“you implore the blue,

& will not tarry,”

hum. this mogul’s got the moth eye.

“imbue acute disquiet.”

> “hw   te   gn   e a l   n d   n d
> sprsf ow   o ul   t sms lo stei r   x pp h w
> t h e   o l y   r e h l few e l e g   s dn
> l i   ke a m   i l e   o   t   fl ur   sssh
> nd   h e r o se   b ls d   i c k
> s li f t   d p y ”

no sycophant,

Though I dig yr kaolin
                dental work/

You may not borrow
     my cat-
          ions,

          “I will trade you
     no-
thing for yr golden

rows of soughing light,”

I am like the lithe autumn dust

I am sewn into yr gasoline,
          “yr sleeping chamberlain

was a symptom of a charismatic snow.”

          “your wheezing is more indicative than
          your fountains’ gloaming
               pomp, which is gross,”

yr capital ripping-
       hook is telling me that
       every ballad has club banger potential:

              If My Hand Is On Your Labia
              (Does That Qualify, As Kissing You?)

a sleeping fountain bleeding,

       "all that touch"

       "it was illusion."

              A peaceful refraction
                     yes,

       yr wet dream was a moral technicality,

       "you are weaker than yr reflux,"

              yr seed is like yr cenotaph,

       in that;

       they
          both ex-
       ist

   in the pit of
the perfume
of yr vo
       ice,

              Unbuttoning yr embers

              //slow roll//

              slurping this   a dead AA,
       a terminal seismic   ru-
              pture;

       another drain_type/

fiddles playing nothing

//RESOUND//

in that I carry my soul
in the form of a pocketed coin,

    in that the fluid of a an ogle
        wields a window/

           yr opening was a black
        voile balcony,

        opening out

onto a garden of a certain sequined poplin,

        opening out

from the inside of a cabinet
        made of oak/

        "I was in my grosgrain bodice."

           u were in an offline
         circular room to be sure,

    in the inside

    of an old castle.

III

The Mariner

        Still the center holds
      the catafalque,
    holds a polymer concrete from wastes
        and Recycled Poly(ethylene terephthalate)
          coffin
      holds
a princess holding a vile
          of lily aldehyde.

"Assume then,"

      "that yr alabaster was in truth
a collagen-like lip injection yes"

      it is customary/

      this firing
      of a warning-
        shot."

      "iCon."
we r burning Gel at each
      one of yr poly-
      tope's efferves-
          cent corners,

          it was all
          we could do
          to grieve well,

    in other words

there was a single viewing window

      //frame shift//

      two hills approaching distance,

there was a spoonful
of a salt-
    free broth

at the bottom
    of it all.

        There was a door
        beside a very wooden war-
            drobe;

        curiously,

        "there was only some of yr sub-
cutaneous fascia inside,"

            in other words now

    it must be of a pre-
            pubescent chortle-
        fest,

yes.

    "she was a
sleepover-
        excuse
    4 sure,"

    she was our prom-
        week church lock-
    in with a fake dead doll
    ' d up bo-
        dy.
            shock-
    tart Terror
        -ism©
                there was a dim trace of an ab-
            stinent Diana,

    in other words,

yr tapers lack fume,

            Incant,

    I am melding already.

"They made you out to be an image
Macro,"

CO
on the low,

"the question is when."

"he totally had a bel-
fry in his po-
cket,"

DONG!

"so?"

"did you suck his bandwidth?"

"just before morning,"

awwwwwwwwwwwwwwwwwww

;;;)

"it was when he said
he loved me

most,"

it was so black out

that

//diacritic choke//

BFF!!1!
"let's remember together,"

no.

ergo
she de-
tagged
her-
self†

a vigilant Farce-
                Maneuver,

        "u armed yr bomb
            behind yr back,"

        it was always a novel
clear stiff gel candle payload†

    "you were always com-
        promising yr hydro-
            carbon oil by one or
    more hydrogenated tri-
            block copolymers of a thermo-
                plastic rubber sequence"

            //interstitial pop//

"Is this invention related to candles in the form of firm gels,
        and more specifically, to stiff heterophilic
thermally reversible mineral oil gels,
        preferably white oil gels?"

            why of course
                the
        candles of
        this invention con-
            tain block copoly-
        mers
and blends thereof,

        "the copolymers being preferably
        derived from styrene-
rubber block
        units,"

        the candles are naturally
            transparent and uncolored.

    The gelatinous elastomer composite
exhibits a novel comb-
            ination of properties in-
cluding unexpectedly low pro-
            cessing temperature,

high elongation and tensile strength,
and excellent shape re-
tention after extreme de-
formation under high velo-
city impact and stress
conditions such as three teenage girls

//COPULA//

"sweeeeeeeeeeeeeeeeeeeeeeet!!"

awwwwwwwwwwwwwwwwwwwwwwwwwwwwwwwwwwww

semi-colon
close paren-
thesis,

cuteness with a Q,

I was re-
inventing yr avatar
identity

//CLAIM//

I claim the ornamental design for a
mirr-ored poetry display.
as shown and as
described.

FIG. 1 is a front view of a three-panel
mirrored poetry display;

FIG. 2 is a rear view of a three-panel
mirrored poetry display;

FIG. 3 is a top view, for which the
bottom
view is substantially the same;

//COPULA//

yr sopping eventide,

"my daddy's lawn was danker."

   in other words
 I sat inside a window weaving;

on a good-
  day, I cou-

ld make-
  out an is-
land out there,

     "and it wasn't out of happiness,"

   it was a method of forming and extending the width
of an existing sand beach by raising the level of the beach.

"The method you included in-
    cluded notes on the construction of a barrier,"

"yes, preferably from concrete,"

     "in a configuration having a cross
 section in the form of a substantially equilateral triang-
le,"

     but with a rounded apex at the tip†

     "The barrier is to be cons-
  tructed at a low
tide water level,"

     when the apex is approximately
12 to 18 inches below the high tide
water level.

            As water flows
         over the barrier,

         to the high tide
         level, sand is de-
       posited on the land
            side of the barrier and builds up to the level of the apex†

"The process can be expedited"

    yes by dredging
and pumping sand
  and sea water over
the barrier as the sand builds up to the level of the apex
        on the land side†

              "sand also is deposited on the ocean side,"

  Thereby totally submerging the barrier
so that the barrier does not interfere
  with bathers
or sea turtles
        or the like

        //COPULA//

      no atomic c-
   lock,

"c I bit in-
    2 an ir-
      on sam-
pan of
   God u c,"

     yes but yr mouth is st-
   ill corr-
        oding,

though I don't really taste
  the arugula flavoring
        u advertize.

      "And then a liquid
    or a gel then filled
   their expanded
hollow micro sphere composite beads,"

                    They can be used

              Or chilled prior to use.

      "The liquid or gel is chosen ycs"

so as to
            be able to
                    retain the cold
                or heated temperature
        for the substantial period of time where-
        by the beads can transfer
            the heat or cold
        to the human body over
                a period of time.

    "sisters. to me
this is always any kind of dark."

        it is elongated,

    like flexible string.

like a plurality of round elements/

            "each of said elements being comprised
        of a hollow shell of plastic material
capable of containing a liquid therein
        without the same leaking
to the exterior thereof"

each of said elements being mounted on said string
        and being spaced apart from each other.

        "A congealable liquid is contained within
                each of said elements, it is conventionally
        employed by first inserting all the beads
            into the rectal canal,
                        passed the sphincter
    muscle,
            leaving only the loop or finger ring
        exposed."

    A lubricant
or the like may be ut-
    ilized with the beads

in order to aid in the in-
    sertion process;

during sexual activity and particularly when experiencing orgasm,

     the beads are removed by pulling on yr choke-
    chute,

"in other words
I am claiming to know
  of yr subduction,"

  it had a certain cerebro-
vascular chord structure,

         in other words
       it was growing dim;

       it's coming,
              isn't it?

     like next year's poppies

       //COPULA//

"omg what else did he say?"

    did he say anything about me?

   "Nothing personally, nothing matter of fact,
nothing in a null subject
       language,"

 in other words
it was characterized by its large and full pink-
  colored flowers; early flowering habit;
   fragrant flowers; strong calyxes which resist
    splitting; good postproduction longevity with flowers
maintaining good substance and color
     for more than two weeks in
an interior environment;

   "oh and it's resistant to Fusarium oxysporum."

   "In other words
      yr cultivar
has not been observed under all
  possible environmental conditions."

                in other words,

the phenotype may vary somewhat with variations
        in environment such as temperature,
daylength,
        light intensity,
                and water and nutritional status without,
however,
                any variance in genotype

                //COPULA//

        something traditional.

        in other words yr impending light of regret†

                it was a high-
        octane moral high-
                road,

and second,

    I didn't vote
to have it put to sleep,

                "o no
                o not
                an-other
                Dexedrine
                        Dose,"

        yr history is full of soft tissue damage

in fact,
                it was worse than we initially thought
    it was.

                concentrate Pierrot.

        rattle yr lead
low register fingerings and blow,

                forgetting not to tell us
        how u feel about it,

entertaining us/

"I was the coif of an atmospheric
        filibuster,"

marco polo me.

why?
                precisely,

            u r a LASIK cheap-
                fix,

so whorl me;

    Why whistle-blower,

"do you appreciate the way I
        am bending forward?"

I was cupping her palms / across his kneecaps,

    I was just saying/

                u were not the first to do so,

        I was just saying,
            in other words

                somewhere near
            my mother's house,

            nearby   there   was   a
        babbling broo-
            k,
                She was a palm-reading
        Charlatan Detector,
                            note;
                                    the un-
        quavering nature of her poly-
            graph   electro-
        encephalograph
            -y was actual-
        ly her fear of her

god/

she was born in the wake of your wave
pool techno-
cracy;

at three months, she was chlorinated by the father
of some per-
formative under-
taker, she
miscarried in
to an under-
tow,

"my angel wore the reddest most hydro-
dynamically efficient swimsuit on the market,"

it was the first time I could
really remember getting wet/

o whistle-blower.
"don't stop trying to resuscitate
me,"

speak
into
my non-
xenophobic
Eustachian
Valve please,

"speak slow, ok?"

//critical point//

a cold synæsthetic keep,

FIG. 1 is a front, right, top perspective
view of the new ornamental plasma
screen of the present invention;

FIG. 2 is a rear view thereof;

FIG. 3 is a left side view thereof;

FIG. 4 is a right side view thereof;

FIG. 5 is a top view thereof;

FIG. 6 is a bottom view thereof;

FIG. 7 is a rear, right, top perspective view thereof,

"it was choppier than normal"

//static snow//

subjecting our ship to a squall
line,

"I was only really apprehensive
of the water's high sodium
content,"

we r waiting for u
2 unlock the door,

were bored/

we want out,

"Barns!
take a letter!"

how about a
U?

negative, that's 2:

"better make it about all of us"

"when in the Course of human events
we do not jump ship,"

"we take the yoke back!"

"we didn't jump!"

"wc didn't have time!"

"we took back the bridge!"

//cæsura//

We asked our most optimistic able
seaman on hand
to a-
ssess
our structural damage,

"the hull is half-
empty of water,"

the environment is against us

//bailing out//

waiting for a fresh injection of liquidity,

orogenic eunoia,
eustatic
Redivac.

File corruption/
Reinstalling...

morning tapering/
capillary action...

"no more vapor."
"no more vigil."

IV

13 Sonnets

As two
  as hands
    their dorm
the lake
    incensed;

    and skin
        as à
      la mode
      destroyed,
low cause.

Unseen
    in me
      mean all
          mine was
              procured;

what me
    resigned
      am Sir
          sob ray
      to man
      extends.
"Bag of
    meant un-
      seen sob
          ray o
      silence,
farther."

Combat
    end o
      delight,
          it is

though a
    czar, new
      attack!

  And the
      note ka

        me ka
      thee o
    Egypt
      am I
              holy,
heart?

      "Noose your
        braces

              in cruise,"
sepulchres
    in Karnak.

        Fair cache,
              the Pharaoh's
    risen
      mummie's
          roads...
Tubas
    am I
      finesse
          am bronze
the toads,

                A peg
          and o
      say I
    am sins,
              ahem,
        "lamp add
      us some
breeze us."

                And to
          adore
    may cede
    of a
                tanto
          tempo,
    "I am
        pronto."

Oozes seas

                    in the   embrangled
               lake   tanto,
          Case is
                         case
          err
               corpse gnash
                    too as
                         thin hands.

                         New palace.   The peacocks
                    sound a pen as dizzy loss.   As as as.
                         Chord o long ergo does sober meme. Exist
               in the peacocks.   O my sin. Tear me a vellus   and
          o my son are you allayed?   Sound lakes on gardens.   When
     passed on park, I in country Nitokris.   Via feet.   Hey as hands
          pare a power   sin as purple as. My eyes form snow
                    I am waters intranquil
               as my senses.   Snail nose dead dozed Nitokris.
          Labyrinth of suns.   Adore me sew me gold. Unsee.   Turned
     off.   God leafs my soul in gold.   My eyes part see.   Arcades,
                    noses spell use.

          Raises what?

               Noon cave end.

          Halitosis,
               the sow is dead.

     As two as hands,
     "how large?"
               "Hung in to divine."

Dad is.

                    Seize, ma'am.

     (Ibis)   (pagans:)

     sober tap,

                    "it is values."

Limb roam in tone of meme raise of me long. Seismochronograph.
And o remembrance me of mine so ooze my passus passed.

Archaism blew my proper mysticism
      And I am left a pen as Corps work vitreous, lost.

            "O your breath is light in candelabras, vellus."
                  The cantos does rooms wave me let me see.
                  And your passus of Pain; sew the shattered mirror.
                  "When you care o see, more's on my to see."

            Open some shore and oh. O yore more hair,
      Golden ash in tulle,

            "ardency, o antiquity,"
E o tear tea see more ta,
                  o me do dee pair dare me.

            "Procure o me,
in silence o e oh ee Sew me in your Steps."
            Sober altar is Pagan. Ergo,
                  I divine am Dead
                  And Isis, lease me my Sayer I am Curtained
                        owing lassos.

Extended us me us brace us for a   brace are you
And enter news won adore say you shut   up.

A puff of air of rubies in my flight,
Puff of air let the powders dream you up.

I left to your shadow plastic windows
And it lost them, how large, the groves of trees...

Hose my fingers since I rule caravels,
They were prolonged extensions of your fin   gers.

In the park of olive gardens you I   dreamed
Again though you of a gold that burned me

In thee Amphoræ of the temples of   my Sayer.
I think you I see you are far away...

I   removed me from me to be alone...
            My eyes sew a sun braid of you to see!

I   see walking in the curves of the grove
            A princess many years ago gone mad,

Princess devil Corpus, a grove clearing

I   n principalities of pheasants' ilk.
     And your shade, a lake's blue.
     As your hands conspiring pine tree forests,

I   remember ships always making port,
     Seagulls with no wings in a palace made of silk.
     Your fingers, the nails that nailed into Christ.
     Look at me long. In your gaze I exist...

I   walk in the prayers of an antique mouth...
     Arch me vaulted dreaming about ivory.
     Iamb the arc played with in the garden,
     That princess many years ago gone mad.

Sing to what as two as hands your eyes sound blinded, your eyes that forgetting as speeches of light sound cloisters clicking off steps forgotten the gold how regressed as the rolling papers are Jesus. Sing too as to pluck are plucked the fiddles olden, where the fingers unravel in chords of gold, evensong: you they will blind from sound. And in candelabras burn o your antique looking, framing mirrors. Your fingers all knocking in your hands, sound oars still sea in the rooms of the palace, heaving, as two as hands in Pain try opening the doors. Bus came, o terapixel, and when we missed it walking as two as hands in my fingers, seismic ruptures ivory statues, around the dead arcades,

of their only
rest, the echo

of their roars,
that the vaults

of the chambers

      //return//

   more tapered,

as rent as what usury made sleepy,

their mouths and as wrinkles know

     your face

       about to,

       deep fall.

No end to park in,

  a dead half gull,

you guarded yr silence

   as razed

as broke stones.

     Usury in

    an-
other time
     yr eyes' dormant.

u quit
usury,

and yr eyes

     will burn the Color of your hands
     in the crossings of other westward

suns.

     blind from me.

     broke.

And when u returned

    (soiled from Distance),

  that my senses were always pine trees

flanking the road the road you walked!

lakes sleep   your shadow
 as palace doors   a gesture,
sheets falling   fingers cold.
 streets dead,

streets were   who are you
 distant were
your hands   to sleep
 were sleeping,   above rivers.
  Salomé   gone
  bronze the westward sun in red veils—
  , far away,
your Body,

  Salomé your brown hands
   of silk,unveiled
    your   breath
And Body   barely a curve.

  Salomé your eyes,
   afraid
  drinking light from the light of your eyes...

  Salomé † maybe asleep...
Maybe   Absent...
Maybe kissing the hands of God...

  God,   docks where others
      dont exist.
 vitreous.
Heaving their lungs

   tableau in your tired hands,
       never erected.
 lips   in lighter,
  descending.

She and God John's body.
   Sleeping bronze of speech,
And shade   of palm.

   Still. And God in your
long wings, embroidered capital,
     ~~air~~————————
      ~~falling~~
             ~~framed~~!

Tall candles they tapered

back   yr lipid grudge u

blew it Out usurped the

veneration of a bone went

straight for yr Smoke it

was asleep that readies

dreams.

In the awakening, I sense the colors, at night,
will be scared and will yoke themselves to the
shadows of your crape. I was a King Goth,
where in Toledo the Tagus River went all sleepy
and I still hear it.

     Inlaid in gold, the rooms I inhabited,
     Golden embers forgotten, dormant gold.
     And in my Soul, in which I am still king

Thrones tremor falling bit by bit.
I seek out the sad pages of my paths.
And my legend in vellum dreams
Goes on writing in silence my tremors.

     They are others the dominions in which I lived
     All the things that I formerly saw
     Returned mysteriously to my sight.

When you I saw I went to your flight

And descended God to me to meet in me.
He flew me over bridges of ivory—
And one of the bridges, God, in my sight!

He haloed me in gold in shadows cold
And my flights fell destroyed.
They were feelers of God my senses.
My Body moved in the lap of Mary.

Now sleeps Christ in pagan veils.
They are carpets of God my hands.
Returns Anxiousness to catch the skies.

He lifts me more. I am the profile of Pain.
Above the arms of God I look around
And God doesn't know which of us is God†

V

Ducted Frieze Vents

An artificial turf of the invention
        is disclosed
            in which
        tufts of artificial
    glass filaments
    are implanted
        on a backing
                structure
        to perform a pile surface,

and tufts of assist filaments,

    which are shorter than
        the artificial glass filaments,

are implanted between the tufts of the artificial glass filaments.

            This construction

            prevents the artificial glass
                filaments from folding
        for a long period of time
                since the assist filaments
                support the artificial glass filaments,
so that a soft and resilient feel
                resembling natural turf
            can be obtained.

When using longer lengths of artificial glass filaments,

    it is possible to obtain an appearance similar to natural turf
and to enhance sliding characteristics on a turf surface,

whereby sliding actions in a soccer game or the like can be performed readily.

            //furthermore//

        in the case of providing a sand layer over the backing cloth
                with the tips of the artificial glass filaments projected
        from the surface of the sand layer,

the obtained artificial turf
                maintains a softness
                        suitable for use in courts,

                    playgrounds or the like
                              for a long period of
                              deranged drainage, Pierrot,
               it was a blood feud machination,
          an intracellular sleep, osmotic pressure, hydo-
                    electrolysis, a rare divorce from yr occidental vagrancy,
     inductive fallibility, mud nest, a glomerular pre-
          ventative embankment, a raging juxt-
       aglomerular apparatus,
            an aerial feeding polydipsia,

     ideologically based violence,
          silence,

          in the form of a convoluted tubule smooch.
               spells courtship

          //lunar squawk//

               "Living in an autogamic pit"
                         —Fuck.

               His waking up was a relative elongation;
               Pandiculation at best.

VI

Sestina

one   I
        my   of
say   feeling,

feeling
of
I
say
my
one

one
say
of
feeling
I
my

my
feeling,
one
say
of
I

I
one
feeling
my
say
of

of
my
one
I
feeling
say

say
I
my
of
feeling
one.

VII

P-N Junction

It with a for a for a faith in,
and a for in, and an idea
to an in an old It. Part of
a plan. And it a single thing
to do with That was just
a goof. To his sure, his
on the wall. And a that
little has into and all around
the world. That has into the,
from to the to and its own in,
as in, and the ship having been
     sunk.

     bloop.

VIII

Sailor_Mouth

For the affect is not a personal feeling, nor is it a characteristic; it is the effectuation of a power of the pack that throws the self into upheaval and makes it reel.

—D&G

Thinks alone in desert pier, morning of summer,
Eye prò-side of bar, eye prò-infinity,
Eye and confines I see,
Black and clear, a pack entering.
Comes far, clear, classic in its own way.
Let air far behind you, edge of his vain smoke.
Come entering, and morning he enters, and rivers,
Here, there, agrees to life at sea,
Brace up candles, moving tugs,
There are small boats behind ships that are in port.
There is a wave breeze.
But my soul is what I see less.
With packs that enter,
Because he is the distance, with Morning,
With sense of maritime Time,
With painful sweetness rises nausea,
A start to fill, but in spirit.

Eye far the pack, a great independence of spirit,
And within me a steering wheel begins to rotate, slowly.

Packages that come, that morning's bar,
Reflect to my eyes
The joyful and sad mystery who comes in part.
Reflect distant memories of pier and other moments
Otherwise, the same humanity elsewhere.
All berth, every drop of ship
It is I feel it in me as my blood...

Ah, the entire pier is a nostalgia stone!
And when the ship wide the pier
Rots and if repair, which suddenly opened up a space
Between pier and ship,
And comes to me, I do not know why, recent anguish,
Missed feelings, sadness,
What glitters in the sun is my distress, grassy
As the first window where the morning beats
And involves me in a remembrance, another person,
What was mysteriously mine?

Oh, *who knows, who knows*,
If not participating once before me,
Doom berth, if not left, ship-to-sun
Oblique by morning's drizzles,
Another type_port?

Who knows if not left before, hour
From the outside_world as I see,
Ray up for me.
Large pier full of little people,
Doom, a big city half awakens,
Doom, a huge commercial city; accretion; apoplexy,
As far as this can be, out of the space and the time!

Yes, a pier, a pier, mode_material,
Real, visible as pier, wharf really,
The Pier Absolute by the model unconsciously intimated,
Unconsciously razed,
We All built
Our berth inside our ports,
Our current_berth of stone on water true,
What if constructed after announcing suddenly
Real Things, spirit_Things, Entities in Stone_souls?
A certain moment of our sense_root,
When the world_outside, and that opens a door
And without that nothing will ever change.
All it is multiverse.

Ah the Grand Pier where left in Ships Nations!
The Grand Pier Previous, eternal and divine!
From that port? In that water? And because I believe this?
Big Pier and the other pier, but the One.
Full as they, plangent in the dawns of silences,
And morning unbuttons with the noise of a crane
And arrivals of goods train,
And under the black cloud and occasional mild, and
From the bottom of the chimneys of factories close,
What you shadow, the flour of a coal black child that shines,
As if the shadow of a cloud / that goo on water bleak.

Ah, that essentiality of mystery and meaning stopped
In revealing divine bliss,
Hour color of silences in distress,
There is no bridge between pier and the pier!

Pier oppression reflected in the water_stops,
Murmur on board ships,
Ó soul wrong, unstable and the people who walk loaded,
The people who/semiotic pass/and with whom nothing lasts,
When the vessel returns to port;
There is always any change aboard!

Ó leaks continued, trips, drunk of medley!
Soul eternal of browsers and sailing!
Skulls reflected in the waters, slowly,
When the large ship, the port!
Flotsam of soul and life as voice,
Living the moment, the liquid_termagant. Always.
Agree for days, more direct than the days of Europe.
See mysterious ports on the solitude of the sea,
Turn long_cables to sudden vast landscapes
For countless slopes aghast...

Ah, the remote beaches, the pier Viewed from a distance,
And then the next beaches, the pier viewed closely.
The mystery of each trip and each arrival,
The painful instability and inconceivability,
This impossible universe
And more in each hour, maritime own_skin senses!
The hiccup absurd that our souls pour
About stretches of seas with different islands in the distance,
About the islands of the remote switch\bank left
About the sharp rise of ports, their homes and, their people,
For the vessel approaches...

Ah, the freshness of the morning in which it arrives,
Exit pallor of the morning
When our bodies are thrust forward
And a vague feeling similar to a fear
—Fear ancestral to depart and leave,
The mysterious fear ancestral to Arrive in New—
Contract us, the skin and agony,
And our entire body feels distressed,
As if our soul,
An inexplicable desire to be able to feel that another way:
A nostalgia to anything:
A disturbance of shapes that wave homeland.
What Costa? That ship? That pier?
What is ill in us is thought,
And only is a big vacuum within us,
A hollow satiety of minutes, seafarers,
And a vague anxiety that would be boredom or pain
If you knew how to do so...

The morning of summer is still a little fresh.
A mild drowsiness, evening walks still_shaken in the air.

Accelerates up slightly on the steering wheel within me.
And the pack is entering because, must be entering undoubtedly
And not because I see the move_up in its excessive distance!

In my imagination it is already close; it is visible
In the whole length of the lines of their periphery.
It shakes everything in me, all the meat and all the skin,
Because of that creature that never arrives on any boats
(And I came today expected to berth) for an oblique warrant.

Vessels entering the bar,
Ships leaving the port,
Ships that pass in the distance
(I suppose them seeing them, a deserted beach)—
All these ships almost abstract in their way,
All these ships well_melt me as being something else
And not only ships, vessels going and coming.

And the ships viewed closely, even if it does not embark on them,
Visas low, the boats, high walls of plates,
Visas within, through the chambers, the halls of the expenditure,
Looking close to the masts, pointed up there prò_high,
Cheated by ropes, down the stairs uncomfortable,
Sniff the mixing daubed metal and sea of everything—
Vessels_visas are closely else and the same thing,
They give the same nostalgia and the same eagerness another way.

All the maritime life! Everything in life: sea!
In_still is in my blood all this seduction, fine
And I dislike indeterminacy, the trips'
Ah, the lines of distant shores, the flat horizon!
Ah, the cables, islands, beaches of wire!
The loneliness I see as certain moments in the Pacific,
In that, I do not know why suggestion learned in school
(If you feel the nerves weigh on the fact that He is the greatest of the oceans)
But the world is a taste of things, becomes a desert within ourselves!
The extension more human, more dotted, the Atlantic!
The Indian, the most mysterious of all oceans!
The Mediterranean, sweet, without any mystery, classic, a sea to beat
From meaning looked at the pavement of gardens coming by white statues!
All seas, all close, all bays, all spit,
I narrow them to the chest, felt them well and dying!

And you, or things, shipyards, my old dreams of toys!
Compose out of me my life inside!

Keels, masts and sails, wheels of the rudder, cordages,
Chaminés of vapors, propellers, topsails, banners,
Gales, hatches, boilers, manifolds, valves;
Fell by me in stacks of mountain,
As the contents of a drawer evicted, confused on the floor!
HQ, you the treasure of my feverish greed,
HQ, you the fruit of the tree of my imagination,
Theme from my corners, blood in the veins of what *logos*,
Yours is the milk that unites me to the outside for aesthetics,
Freaks your metaphors' images, literature,
Because in actual fact, seriously, literally,
My feelings are a bloat to keel prò_air,
My imagination an anchor half submerged,
My eagerness a rowing party,
And the tessitura of my nerves, a network to dry on the beach!

Sounds like no chance of the river like a whistle, only one.
Tremor now, the entire floor of my psyche.
To accelerate is increasingly the steering wheel inside me.

Ah, the bellboy travel, it does not know the whereabouts
From bean or bird of such lines, we know!
Ah, the glory of knowing that a man who walked with us
He died drowning at the foot of a Pacific island!
We with him that with him we will talk about it to everyone,
With legitimate pride, with a confidence invisible
In that sense, all this has a more beautiful and wider constituency,
Why only to have lost the boat where he did,
And he has gone to the bottom of it: there has entered water prò_lungs!

Ah, the bellboy, charcoal ships vessels from sailing!
They are paint thinner – woe is me / of me! – Ships from the sailing seas!
And I, I love the modern civilization, I kiss with the soul the machines,
I am the engineer, I was civilized, I was educated abroad,
I would like again to walk in my view, only sailboats and boats of wood
From not knowing another sea life that the old lives of the seas!
Because the seas are a former Absolute Distance,
The Pure Far, free of the weight of the Current...
And ah, like everything here reminds me that lives better
These seas, these better: because we sailed slower.
These seas, mysterious: because they knew less of themselves.

All the steam is distance in a boat sailing nearby.
Every ship seen now is a ship next seen in the past.
All invisible, sailors on board ships on the horizon

Are sailors visible, time of the old ships,
From the time of sailing sailboats, slow and dangerous,
The era of wood and canvas of the trips that lasted months.

Takes me little_by_little, the high of the things nautical,
Penetrate me physically, the pier and its atmosphere,
The tide soughing crossing me on top of my senses,
And I start dreaming, start to involve myself / a dream of water;
They get to take the well_to_transmission belts in my soul,
And the acceleration of the steering wheel shakes me clearly.

They call me by the waters,
They call me by the sea,
They call for me, raising a body of voice, far, far away,
The maritime times all experienced in the past to draw.

You, English sailor, Jim Barns my friend you were,
Let me drill this ancient cry, English,
What you so venomously C
As the soul's complex, as my
calling confusing water,
A voice unprecedented and implicit of all things of the sea,
Two shipwrecks, the travel remote, of dangerous crossings.
That thy cry English, became universal in my blood,
Without affect, to cry without human form or voice,
This tremendous cry that seems sound
From inside a cave whose roof is the sky
And seems to narrate all things disastrous,
What can happen in the Far / in the Sea, the Night...
(Copped where a schooner that was calmed
And well spoken, putting a hand on each side of the mouth
Doing the voice of big hands, blistered and dark:

Ahò-ò ò---ò ò ò---ò ò ò---ò ò-yyyy ...
Schooner ahò--ò ò ò---ò ò ò---ò ò ò---ò ò ò---ò ò - yyyy ...)

Listen you, here, now, and awake to anything.
Dither the wind. Raze the morning. The heat opens.
I polish my nails and faces.
My eyes aware, dilate up.
The bliss in me rises, grows progresses,
And with a nose of blind street riots, accentuates
The spin of the wheel alive.

Ó clamoroso, calling

The heat rich, as fury in me burbles,
In an explosive unit, all my nausea,
My own particulars made dynamic, everyone!...
An appeal launched to my blood,
Doom past love, I do not know where, which involves,
And I still have the strength to attract and pull
What still sail has strength to make me hate this life,
That step between the physical and mental impenetrability,
The real people that live!

Oh, in any case, weather by wear / Form!
Drop So on the waves, the danger, by the sea.
Far to Go, go to "Off" for Distance, abstrAktno,
Indefinite, for the nights' mysterious and deep,
Took such as dust, as grows as gales!
Go, go, go, go every once!
All my blood for rabies wings!
All my body throw up front!
Crimp my imagination out in torrents!
Run me over, roar / precipitate me!...
Outbreak of violet foam in my nausea
And my beef is a wave giving float stone!

Thinking this: your anger! Thinking this: we fury!
Thinking this: the narrow of my life is a full of nauseas,
Suddenly, tremulously, exorbitant,
With a vicious swing_broad violent,
From the steering wheel of my imagination, alive,
Ripped, for me, whistling, sylvan fizz, vertigo,
The heat and somber sadist shrill of life at sea.

Eh captains of ships! They were all at the helm and masts!
They who sleep in bunks abrupt!
They who sleep cool, a peek through the curtains of Danger!
They who sleep cool, Death by pillow!
They who have poop decks, which have bridges, which has attitude,
The vast immensity of the sea immense!
Eh handlers of the cargo cranes!
Eh struck sails, by candlelight, created aboard!
They who stuck the cargo in the holds!
They who wound cables on deck!
They who clean the metal of the hatch!
They of the rudder! They of the machines! They of masts!

010001010110
1000001011

0101100101011

01000001011010
1100101011
010000010110
10110010
101101000
001011010
1100101011
010000010
11010
1100
101
0110
100000
1011
01011
0010101
101000
00100
0010
10101
0001
001
01
1!
People of the pipe,

the knitted sweater!

People of anchors and flags crossed edges in the chest!
People from the main-rail!
People of both dark-sun, defalcation of so_much rain,
Clears the eyes of such immensity before them,
Audacious face of so many winds they fought to assert!

010001010110100000101
101011001010110
100000101101
01100010110
1000001011
010110010

                    10110100
                    0001011
                     01011
                      0010
                        10110
                      10000
              0   1011010
              1   1001
              01 0110
        10 000 010 11010
            110
                  0101
                011010
                    0000
                   100
                 0010
                    010
          00

              0

            0!
They who seen Patagonia!
They who passed Australia!
What fill, you look back that you never see!
What ye land in the land where ye stood never!
What currency articles, gross colonial tundral bow!
And you did all this as if it were not nothing!
As if it were natural,
As if life were so,
Because not even fulfilling a destination!

(Eh
      - (eh
     - (eh
         - (eh
      - (eh
      - (eh - eh)))))));
            !

They of the sea current! They of the sea past!
Commissioners of the bar! Slaves of origin! Combatants from Lepanto!
Pirates of the time of Rome! Browsers of Greece!
Phoenicians! Carthaginians! Portuguese thrown from Sagres
Toward indefinite adventure towards the Sea Absolute, to perform the
            Impossible!. .... ‾....‾ . .... ‾....‾ . .... ‾....‾ .
.... ‾....‾ . .... ‾....‾ . .... !

They who towered standards, that the names of these cables!
They who banked for the first time in the pocket of a black hole's jeans!
What first venerated slaves of new land!
What, the first spasm of the European black_gasp?
What peddled golden sandalwood arrows
From hillsides burst in to green vegetation!
Heart of darkness,
What did escape with the noise of guns these races,
What slay; rounce and robber inquisition; big money
Premiums for New, who, head low,
Catapult against the mystery of new sea! Eh-eh-eh-eh-eh!
To you all in a you all in you all, as one,
To you all mixed, loomed,
To you all bloody, violent, hated, feared, sacred,
I welcome you, I salute you, I salute you!
Eh eh-eh-eh eh! Eh-eh-eh-eh-eh-eh eh! Eh-eh-eh-eh-eh-eh eh!
E h l a h ô- l a h ô l a H O –l a h á w ill wil l_t o_t he!

I want to go with you / I go with you,
At the same time with you all
to everywhere else to ponder ye!
I find your danger face 2 face,
Feel the wind in my face that you're wizened.
Cuspid lips of the salt of the seas that tongued you,
Having Ishmael in your arms, you share your storms,
Getting like you, finally, the extraordinary ports!
Delete your culture!
Loosing upon the concept of morals!
Feel change in the far, my humanity!
Drinking together in the southern seas
New Africas, new babbles of the soul,
New fires in the central volcanic gust!
Go you, take my clothes off - ah! Puts on your get-out-of-here!—
My beauty of civilized, my mild actions,
My innate fear of chains,
My peaceful life,
My life seated, static, and a ruled magazine!

In the sea, the sea, the sea, the sea,
Put in the sea, the wind, the waves:
My life
Of foam thrown by the winds, saline, salient!
My taste of the big trips.
Whipper_water_whipper, the meat of my adventure,
On_and_on cold ocean of the bones of my existence,

Disaster; caliper; crop; crimp of winds, foams, suns:
My cyclone be the Atlantic:
My nerves post as shrouds_of_ships,
Dollars in the hands of a psycho!

Yes, yes, yes ... Stuck me in the sailing
And my backs enjoy my sticks!
A necktie travels on the mast, whipper,
And the feeling of masts comes by my spine
And I, going to feel them in a large coming passive:
Do what you will to me, once that is in the seas.
Around decks, to the sound of waves,
Let me cry, kill, almost!
What I want to is prò_Death,
A soul, sable spill over the Sea;
Cirrhoses, the fall of the things nautical;
Both of townsfolk as anchors cables,
Both the coasts remote as the noise of winds
Both the Far as the Pier, both of shipwrecks
As the quiet shops,
As far as the masts are the vacancies,
Bring prò_Death with pain, tits,
A cup full of leeches, sugar, sugar,
From strange green sea leeches absurd!

Skeleton ships of my veins!
Mooring lines of my muscles!
Slice me to the skin, preach it to the keel.
And I can feel the pain of the nails and never stop feeling!
Is my heart of a stamp collection, Admiral?
In time, the war of old ships
Tread on foot decks in my eyes, away!
Break me of the bones to meet the catwalk!
Spank me tied to the mast, spank me!
To all the winds of all latitudes and longitudes,
Comes of gob & blood on water_tossed,
What crossing, the ship, the deck, a kind of side_by_side
In squalls to brave the storm!

Having the audacity to wind the clothing of candles!
Being such as crows nests, whistle of the upper_winds!
The old blues guitar of the seas / full of dangers,
Download of the Day!

Sailors / that milt,

Noosed the captain / up in a wicker embalm.
Terra firma, another island desert.
Marooned! Marooned!
The sun of the tropics has a fever of piracy, degree_roe
In my veins' intensive.
The winds of Patagonia, ink of my imagination
From tragic and obscene signified
Fire, fire, fire, within me!
Sangue! Blood! sangue! Blood! sangue! Blood! sangue! Blood!
Explode all my brain!
It is to me the world in red!
Blow me with the sound of tethers tethers the veins!
And click me on fierce, greedy,
The song of the Great Pirata,
The death of the Great (shout) Pirata to sing
Until a measure of fear plies bones from his men below.
There's re: to die, and screen to sung:

Fifteen men on the Dead Man's Chest.
Yo-ho ho and a bottle of rum!

And then shouting in a voice already unreal, in the air crash:

Darby M'Graw-aw-aw-aw-aw!
Darby M'Graw-aw-aw-aw-aw!
Fetch aa-aft the ru-uuuuuuu-mmm, Darby.

Yo, that this life! That was the life, yo!
Eh-eh-eh-eh-eh-eh-eh!
Eh-lahô-lahô-laHO-lahá will will-to-the!
Eh-eh-eh-eh-eh-eh-eh!

Extension of brow to stern, departure, ships to the bottom, blood in the seas!
Convivial fill of blood, of fragments of bodies!
Fingers chipped on catwalks!
Heads of children here, there!
People of eyes_out, shouting howl!
Eh-eh-eh-eh-eh-eh-eh-eh-eh-eh!
He-he-he-he-he-he-he-he-he-he!
Fold me in all this as a layer cake, batter in the cold!
Rub me, for this is a cat in heat by a wall!
Cry as a hungry lion for all this!
Charge as a crazy bull in all this!
Horns nails, claws delivery; bleed yr teeth into that!
Eh-eh-eh-eh-eh-eh-eh-eh-eh-eh!

Suddenly pop me on the ears,
A clarion in my hand,
The old cry, but now anger; feldspar; biogenic silica *in vivo*,
Calling the prey that you will,
The schooner that will be taken:

Ahó-ó-ó-ó-ó-ó-ó-ó-ó-ó-ó-yyyy...
Schooner ahó-ó-ó-ó-ó-ó-ó-ó-ó-ó-ó-ó-ó- yyyy...

The whole world does not exist for me! Ergo red!
Cry of the fury of an approach!
César-Pirata! César-Pirata!
Foraged weed, ruined tear!
Just feel the sea, the prey, the drawing!
Only feel in me, beat / hit me,
The veins of my scratches / sources!
Score my blood, the cantilevered hot_sensation of my eyes!
Eh-eh-eh-eh-eh-eh-eh-eh-eh-eh-eh!

Oh pirates, pirates, pirates!
Pirates love me and don't me!
Which me_you, pirates! Toss the salad!

Your anger, your cruelty to speak to the blood
Of a body of a woman who was once my rut, and whose survives!

I wanted to be a beast representative of all your gestures,
A beast that cadges teeth. In walks Bulwark, keels over.
What eats masts, blood suckler, and tar on deck,
Rend the sails, oars, rope and polymer,
Sea snake sea and monstrous female fattened up in crimes by her own accord!

And there is a symphony of sensations, an incompatible similar.
There is an orchestration in my blood of fractile misdemeanors,
From din to throe of orgies, from blood into the seas,
Blast as the zeroth heat of the spirit,
Cloud of dust hot petticoat under my light
And making me see and dream it all, only with skein and veins!

The pirates; piracy; boats; time:
That hour sea hour where the prey are subject to a stickup,
And the terror of the capture escapes prò_madness, suck time,
In its total crimes, terrors; boats; peoples, sea, sky, clouds;
Breezes latitude, a longitude of shrill.

I myself, who was in his All, my body in its whole stuff:
What was my body and my blood, capillary accretion,
Fluorescent wound, creeps in meat; unreal in my soul!

Would that be all the crimes? Be all the elements' components'
Two assaults on boats (and a massacre and supranumeral violations)!
Being that was in the place of the drawings!
Being on or lied_lived at the site of the tragedies of blood!
Being the pirate_summary of the whole piracy at its peak,
And the victim_synthesis, but of flesh and bone, all pirates of the world!

Being my body's liabilities, the woman-all-women-as-
What were raped, killed, then injured; druxy_confetti!
Being in my being subdued a female who has to be them
And feel all this - all these things just a time - the spine!

My pilose and abrupt heroes of adventure and crime!
My sea savage beasts, husbands of my imagination!
Lovers of casual obliquity of my feelings!
That I would be that you wait in ports,
To you, your love hated pirates in the blood of dreams!
Because she had you, but only in spirit, pissed
About the naked corpses of the victims who are doing it in the sea!
Because it would have accompanied your crimes, and the ocean gang-
Banging his spirit of a witch would dance, invisible around the gestures
Of your body, your cutlass, arrival of your hands!
And it was ashore, hoping, you when, arrival, if arrival,
It would drink in ruts of your love throughout the vast,
Every foggy accident and the perfume of your winnings,
And through your spasms' fizzled Sabbath of rose and golden gall!
The flesh torn, the flesh open and striped, blood running!
Now, at the height concise dreaming of what you were doing,
Damage me all of me, because you do not belong and I am you,
My femininity, you that accompanies it be your souls!
Being inside of all your ferocity, when practicable!
Sugar inside your awareness of your feelings
When blood engrained the high seas,
When on occasion fed to vegan sharks
The bodies of the wounded still_alive, the pink chaff of children
(And brought the mommies to Bulwark to see what would happen)!

Being together in lust in looting!
Being orchid_straightened, symphony of the drawings on you!
Ah, I do not know what, I do not know how I wanted to be with you!
It was not only you to be female, will be the females, will be the victims,

Be you the victims: men, women, children, ships;
It was not only a time, and the boats in the waves,
It was not only your souls, your body, your anger, your possession,
It was not only specifically your act of abstract excess,
It was not only what I wanted to be - was more that the God_this!
That must be God, the God of a cult to the contrary,
A monstrous and sado_God, a God of a pantheism of blood
To fill the entire extent of my imagined fury,
To never exhaust my wishes of identity
With each, and all, and moor_it_all of your winnings!

Ah, I cut myself to restore myself, smoke
My meat - make it the air that your cross cajoles, cradles
Before fall on the head and shoulders!
My veins are the facts that infiltrates knives!
My imagination, the body of raped women!
My intelligence_deck, where the killers are standing!
My life as a whole nervous, hysterical absurd,
The great organism that each act of piracy that is committed
Was a conscious cell - and all I whirl
As a huge waving root, and what it was!

Such speed disproportionate, stupid_fast,
The machine of fever of my visions that
Turn now that my conscience, steering wheel,
It is just a circle shrouded whistling in the air.

Fifteen men on fhe Dead Man's Chest
Yo-ho ho and a bottle of rum!

Eh-lahô-lahô-laHO - láhá will-ááá - ààà ...

The savagery of this savagery! Merda Shit
prò_whole-life such as ours, that this is nothing!
I here am an engineer, practical to the force, sensitive to everything
I here am stopped, for you, even when walking;
Even when garlic, inert; even when I sandbag, weak;
Static, broken; dissident cowardice of your glory
From your great momentum_stark, hot and bloody!

For failing to act in accordance with my delirium!
Always walking, seized by the skirts of civilization!
For floor with their backs *douceur des moeurs*, as a burden of rent!
Kids the corner - we all are - thc modcrn humanitarianism!
Fever_tizzy, neuromatic lymph,

Without courage to be people with violence and boldness squared,
With the soul as a chicken, pray for a leg!

Ah, the pirates! The pirates!
The eagerness of illegal attached to the fierce,
The eagerness of the things absolutely abominable and cruel,
What tape as an abstract pate of our bodies goffered sinews,
Our nerves' women and banked sensitive,
And puts great fevers, mad in our empty eyes!

Required me to kneeling before you!
Humbled me and knocks!
Bring to me your slave_drive / your thing!
And that your contempt for me never leave me,
Ó gentlemen! Ó gentlemen!

Taking always gloriously part submissive.
The events of blood and the licentious sponge_token!
Acclivity about me, as major heavy walls,
Ó barbarians of the former March!
Lacerations and discord!
Hurt from east to west from my body
Risked the blood of my flesh!
Kissed what minced aboard and lashings and anger,
My joyful terror; cupidity, you belong.
My eagerness_masochist, in giving me to your anger,
In be inert and bilge of your omnivorous cruelty,
Lord you emperors are chargers!
Ah me, Gitmo,
Laceration_boil and open me!
Undone pieces aware out of measure,
Spilled me on the decks,
Spread me in the seas, lead me
Into edacity, the private beaches of the islands!

A wooden duck about me all my mysticism of you!
Hew the blood for the vapors'
Cut! Smudge_stick!
Ó mark of death inside a vacuum!
Erasured love of my crystal submission!
Submitted who me how anyone who kills a dog by over_kicking it!
Bring me to the well of your contempt_domain!

Bring to me your victims' all!
As Christ suffered for all men, I suffer.

For all your victims to your hands,
At a dot on the map your hands and bloody fingers severed
In sudden assaults of the main_rail!

Bring anything from me as if I were
Fatigued - or pleasure, O smooch_pain!
Wore_out the tails of horses tressed for you...
But this at sea, this in the ma-aa-air, that in the MA-AA-AR!
Eh-eh-eh-eh-eh!   Eh-eh-eh-eh-eh-eh-eh!
EH-EH-EH-EH-EH-EH!   In the MA-A-AA-AR!

Yeh eh-eh-eh-eh-eh! Yeh-eh-eh-eh-eh-eh! Yeh-eh-eh-eh-eh-eh-eh!
Cry everything! All shouting! Winds, waves, boats,
Tide_squall, pirates my soul, the blood, and air. And air!
Eh-eh-eh-eh! Yeh-eh-eh-eh-eh! Yeh-eh-eh-eh-eh-eh!
Everything sings shouting!

FIFTEEN MEN ON THE DEAD MAN'S CHEST.
YO-HO-HO AND A BOTTLE OF RUM!

Eh-eh-eh-eh-eh-eh-eh! Eh-eh-eh-eh-eh-eh-eh! Eh-eh-eh-eh-eh-eh-eh!
Eh-lahô-lahô-laHO-OO-ôô-lahá-á á - ààà!
Eh-lahô-lahô-laHO-OO-ôô-lahá will be - ààà!
AHÓ-O-O-O O O O O O O O - yyy! ...
SCHOONER AHÓ-O-O-O-O-O-O-O-O-O - yyyy! ...

Darby M'Graw-aw-aw-aw-aw-aw!
DARBY M'GRAW-AW-AW-AW-AW-AW-AW!
FETCH AA-AFT THE RU-UUUU-MMM, Darby!

Eh-eh-eh-eh-eh-eh-eh-eh-eh-eh-eh-eh eh!
EH-EH EH-EH-EH EH-EH EH-EH EH-EH-EH!
EH-EH-EH-EH-EH-EH-EH-EH-EH EH EH-EH!
EH-EH-EH-EH-EH-EH-EH-EH-EH-EH-EH-EH!

EH-EH-EH-EH-EH-EH-EH-EH-EH-EH-EH!

It is in me anything. The red darkening.
Others felt to be able to continue to feel.
Drained to the last drop, to me the soul, it was only an echo within me.
Ungrew roughly the speed of the steering wheel.
Take me, a little hand of the eyes of my dreams.
Within me there is a single vacuum, a desert, a sea_night.
And as soon as I feel that there is a sea night within me,
You know the distance, Him; he was born of his silence

Again, against the vast_ancient_cry.
Suddenly, a lightning sound, which makes no noise but tenderness,
Suddenly covering the entire horizon, see?
Húmid and human tempest_gloomy night,
Voice of a distance aureoles crying, calling,
It comes from the bottom of Far, from the bottom of the Sea, the soul of Dawn.
Dawn. Down.
And it afloat, such as algae; floats disrupted my dreams...

Ahò-ò ò—ò ò ò—ò ò ò—ò ò - yy ...
Schooner ahò ò—ò ò ò—ò ò ò—ò ò ò—ò ò - yy ......

Ah, the dew on my excitement!
The cool night in my ocean_interior!
That everything in me is before me suddenly, one night at sea,
Full of mystery, humaníssimo, huge_wave_night.
The moon rises on the horizon,
And my happy childhood agrees, as a tear_down_me.
My past resurfaces, as this cry, see?
There was a smell, a voice, the echo of a song;
What was called to my past
For that happiness, that never would spill to have.

It was quiet in the old house next to the river ...
(The windows of my bedroom, and the house_to_dinner also,
They gave, so on some houses, next to the river,
For the Tagus, the same Tejo, but elsewhere, more below ...
If I now come to the same windows not enough to the same windows.
That time has passed as the smoke of a steam on the high seas ...)

An inexplicable tenderness,
A remorse, lachrymogenic, and how,
For all those victims - mostly children—
What I dreamt the dream making me old, pirate,
Emotive prò_morph, tectonic because they were my victims;
Tender and because they were not really;
A confusing tenderness, a tarnished bluish glass,
Sang the old_guard in my poor old soul.

Ah, how could I dream those things?
What I am far when I was a few moments!
Hysteria of crash_sensitivity - sometimes these, or the opposite!
In blonde morning, rising, as my ear only picks:
Things agree with this emulsion - the violet churn,
The violet churning mild of the river to meet the pier...,

A candle passing near the other side of the river,
The distant hills, a blue_Chinese boxes of
What's softness in an infancy at the time of the mourning!...

A gull that passes;
And my tenderness is greater.

But all this time I was not a remedy for anything.
This was only an impression of the skin_like fondling,
All this time took no eyes of my distant dream,
From my house next to the river,
From my childhood next to the river,
The windows of my bedroom onto the river at night,
And the peace of moonlight sparse waters!...
My old aunt, which I loved because of the child who lost...,
My old aunt used sleeping singing me, me
(Although I was already grown too much for that) ...
I remember in tears, fall on my heart and wash_in of life,
And rises on a light sea breeze within me.
Sometimes she sang the *S.S. Nantucket.*

There will the *S.S. Nantucket*
Form on the waters of the sea...

And sometimes, in a melody very late and as medieval,
It was Infanta Bela. Recall, and the poor old voice rises up within me,
Reminds me I just reminded myself of it later; she loved me so much!
As I was ungrateful for it - and after all that I did in life?
I was the Infanta Bela! I clammed up and she sang:

Since Infanta Bela
In the garden resolved

I opened some eyes and via a window full of moonlight,
I closed them again, and all this was happy.

Since Infanta Bela
In the garden resolved
A comb of gold the hand,
Whose hair was glossed

Over my past of childhood, I went / doll!

Not able to travel toward the past, for that houses and that affection,
And stay there always, always happy child and always!

But all this was the Past, flashlight to a corner of the old street.
Think this makes cold, hunger is the thing unless we can get.
Give me not now remorse - absurd - think about this.
Oh swirling slow unfound of no, no!
Vertigo is tenuous of confusing things in the soul!
Furious departure, as tendered carts line with children praying,
Just great, Circe! Imagine on, the eyes of the senses
Tears, useless tears,
Light breezes of contradiction abraded faces by the soul...

Evoke for a voluntary effort to exit this emotion!
Evoke with a despair_effort, saddle_void,
The song of the Great Pirata, when was dying?

Fifteen men on the Dead Man's Chest.
Yo-ho-ho and a bottle of rum!

But the song is a straight line drawn evil within me...

Afford me and I can draw again before my eyes' on the soul,
Another time, but through nearly some form of a translocase,
The fury of piracy - of slaughter_want, almost the taste of wings
From the useless clubbing of women and children,
Gitmo to Tripoli, and only to be distracted, passengers poor
And the sensuality of queer, and from the things most dear of others,
But this dream_off with a fear of anything breathing me on the neck.
I remember; it would be interesting.
Hanged the children of mothers in sight
(But I am not mean to their mothers),
Bury them alive! on the islands' deserted children of four years,
Taking parents in boats until then, they see
(But quake, reminding me of a child who does not have, and is quiet at home sleeping).

Dated hairdo / a cold eagerness of maritime crimes,
Doom an Inquisition without the excuse of Faith,
Crimes even with reason to be evil and fury,
Invent a cold, not even to injure, or an even prosopyle,
Not even to amuse, but to pass the time,
As to whom does patience sup with in the country, with the towel thrown: first
Grab the other_side of the table after_dinner:
Only the smooth taste of committing transgression abominates
And not by much...
From seasickness to the point of madness and death_by_pain.

But never let it get there...
But my imagination refuses to accompany me.
A call of cold, attention bristles.
And suddenly, suddenly more than the other time, further, deeper,
Suddenly - oh fear for all my veins! no, No,
Oh cold sudden, the door to the Mystery which opened within me and has
become a stream of air!
I remember God, the Transcendental of to be, and suddenly
The old voice of the English sailor Jim Barns with whom I spoke,
mysterious voice from within me, the small things in laps of mother and sisters
Of dryer_tape,
But good is coming from beyond the appearance of things;
Broken larynx, a wireless_deaf made The Voice Absolute,
The Voice Without Beam,
Coming on and within the loneliness, the dark of the seas,
Draws for me...I called...called for me...

Come on mute, as if it were abolished and whether to hear
On/axis, as if sounding here and elsewhere and could not hear,
As a hiccup stifling a light that is erased, a silent breath,
From any part of the area of any place in time,
The crying always_dark, the murmur_fund, and confused:

Ahô--ô ô ô—ô ô ô—ô ô ô---ô ô - yyy......
Ahô--ô ô ô—ô ô ô—ô ô ô—ô ô ô—ô ô - - yyy......
Schooner-ah-ô ô ô—ô ô ô—ô ô ô—ô ô ô—ô ô ô-- - yy.........

Tremelo_gold of the soul_redux, I the Ur...
And suddenly opens their eyes, which had not closed.
Ah, the joy of going out of the dreams of time!
Here again the real world, so good for the nerves la-la-la!
Hey you in this hour, mourning for the entering bellboy; he arrives clearly.

Already I am not a matter which hampers the pack who is far clearly.
Only what is now clear me wash the soul.
Deus ex machina / aseptic condition / crash test,
It is only concerned with things modern and useful,
With ships, cargo, with the bellboy and passengers,
With the strong things immediate, modern, commercial, real.
Mitigate its spin within me & the steering wheel.

Wonderful modern surf life,
All cleaning, machinery and health!
Everything arranged as well as spontaneously adjusted,
All parts of machinery, all ships by sea,

All elements of the business of export and import
So wonderfully combing Through,
Which is all as if by natural laws,
Where is the zeroth degree collision with another!

Nothing lost the poetry. And now there is a moor of machining
With his poetry too, and the whole new kind of
Commercial life, multinational corporation dialogue,
That was the machinery; it has brought it to the souls.
The trips now are so beautiful as they were before,
And a ship is always beautiful, but because it is a ship, it needs a makeover.
This is version 2.012, travelling is still travel far
And is always where you were—
Nowhere, thank God!

The ports full of vapors of many species!
Small, large, in various colors, with various provisions of the guard,
In so many, deliciously the shipping!
Vapors in ports, as highlighted by the separation of individual anchorage!
So obsequious your quiet clothes trading things that go into the air,
In March in old Ulysses!
Look, humanitarian of lighthouses in the distance of the night,
Or the sudden lighthouse near the very dark_lite,
(What, we were close to the earth moving!? And the sound of water
Sings our ears off)!...

All this is now as it has always been, but there is trade;
And the fate of the large commercial vapors,
A strutting of the cob!
The mixture of people on board of passenger ships
Give me the pride of modern living in a time where it is so easily
Mixed up in the race, crossing up the spaces; easily see all things,
And enjoying life or doing a lot of dreams.

Clean as regular, as a modern office with gadgets in networks of IEEE 1394,
My feelings now, natural as restraint as gentlemen,
They are practical, far from impractical, fill the lungs of the ocean_breeze,
As people well aware of how hygienic breathe can be, the air of the sea.

The day is now perfectly ours of work.
Everything starts to move, to regulate its selves.
With a great natural pleasure and direct go_around with the soul
All trade, needed for a shipment of goods.
My season is the stamp that leads all invoices,
And I feel heavy that all the cards of all offices

They should be addressed to me.

A knowledge of the board has so much individuality,
And a signature as master of ship is so beautiful and modern!
Rigor trade of principle and the end of the letters:
Dear Sirs - *Messieurs* - Friends and Masters,
Yours faithfully ... The business of salutations...
This is not only humane and clean, but also beautiful,
And the end is a destination of sea, a vapor where aboard
The goods and the letters and invoices, deal?

Complexity of life! Invoices are made by people
(What is love, hatred, passions, policies, sometimes crimes?)
It is so well written, so aligned as independent of all this!
Some people look at an invoice and do not feel it.
Certainly, certainly; you, César_Pirata, read the sentence!
Is feeling that the tears of humanism?
Come tell me that there is poetry in trade in the office!
Now, she invades on all pores ... Detox ... In this air/sea breathe it,
Why all this? This is the purpose of the vapor, navigate the space
Because the invoices and letters and trade are the principles of history,
And the ships that take the goods by sea are the eternal purpose.

Oh, and travel, travel; recreation / and the other talk,
The travel by sea, where we are all the other_companions'
Doom. A special way, as an unknown sea
It approached the souls and became a moment.
USA! USA! U-S-A! A transitional same; transnational limbo,
A lot of moving on the immensity of the water!
Major hotels in the Infinite, transatlantic oh my!
With a cosmopolitanism prefecture and total never stops at one point
And contains all kinds of costumes, faces, races!

The trips' travelers - many species of them!
So much nationality in the world! So much profession! So many people!
Both diversity and destination can give life;
In the life, after all, always in the background, always the same!
So many curious faces! All faces are curious
And nothing brings so much religiosity as much as to look at people.
The fraternity is ultimately not a revolutionary idea.
It is something that we learn for life outside, where
He has to tolerate everything,
And will find the grace that has to tolerate;
And just about to cry, tenderness is about what is tolerated!

Ah, this is beautiful, all that is human, a quarter_inch jack to
HQ, the feeling is, the socialite spotlight and bourgeois.
So hard and simple as theosophy!
All the phytoplankton and all the upper strata and sun;
Ultimately we educate in human terms.
Poor people! Poor people everyone is!

Pay your bills this time in the body of another vessel;
It is now leaving. It is a tramp-steamer, English,
Very dirty, as if it were a French ship,
With an air of the sympathetic, proletariat of the seas,
Something certainly announced yesterday on the last page of the Times.

Oops. Spilled myself, the poor steam, as humble and as he goes naked,
He seems to have a certain scruple, do not know ask how
Why to be honest person,
An agent is an any_kind of duty.
There he will leave the post in front of the pier where I am.
There he goes quietly, through which were ships
Once...
For Cardiff? For Liverpool? To London? It has no importance.
He does his duty. So we do ours. Bela life!
Good trip! Good trip!
Good journey, my poor friend is casual, which made me favor
The lead with a fever and sadness of my dreams
Restore me to life to look at you and see you through.
Good trip! Good trip! Life is this...

What is apropos is natural as is inevitably morning
In your output from the port of Lisbon, today!
I love you a curious grateful_for_it...
So what? I know what is there! ... Go... Go... Go already...
(With a slight infliction,)
(Tt--t---t----t-----t. ..)
The wheel within me stops.
    — — —— ——

Uh_oh, slow_steam, and is not staying happening...
Moves to me; it is in my view,
Will you from the inside of my heart.
Lose yourself in Far, in the Far, fog of God,
Lose yourself, follow your destination and let me...
Who am I to that chore and interrogate?
Who am I to ask you and you love?
Who am I to disturb me_see_you?
Drop the dock, the sun rises, rises on gold,

Light the roofs of the buildings of the pier,
The whole side of the city shines here...
Party, leave me, it makes you
First, the ship is in the middle of the river, and highlighted scarp,
After the vessel *en route* to the bar, small and black,
After vague_point on the horizon,
Points increasingly to vague on the horizon...,
Nothing then; and only I and my sadness,
And a big city now full of sun
And the time as a real and bare berth, already without ships.
And the slow spin of the crane, as a compass that turns,
Moth in semicircle, I do not know that emotion
In the silence of affect, is the soul...

IX

Vacuum Magnets

Err, no of after the the as
am gold the noon shadows

And on will the ohm of plural act
till the go air the sky those

who tent attempt down eyes
know am clasp my that,

Pollute by murder,

they one they of
dream luster dies?

After of What mellow
noon tries! strange days

in am sky one am
quiet the of rumor ignored?

Syringe! Your flute across nice to
meet you and blood Mirage? this

after em, that legend and the god
noon dementia,

of day right old the god
the dream now exhumed old rock.

A is is me, nymphs! quiet
bell and for the the with

which I on there, am
G-ds put clothes me afraid

of being which as of selfish
not it only hands that desire

of but is shade do see
nymphs; there the I not it

after before and, drowned to of
and I am the bode anxiety

of to so see the of
me see, I on back distance!

I to one the in my
left sleep bit sky the eyes,

I them want open what close,
no I to before thy God!

Nymphs! combing frock the
you're the to pane

of soul the shaded how
my through hour and pretty.

Crowns over over as the
not time me of flowers'

loose but slides of
petals, white hands loves

that at an the
open night like children

that at and kids wool
open night like of pit...

You the of sitting happy
are dream me in laps!

          Amathophobic fate

the that occult
bowls spill smell

of of lip that was
seduction tedium caps which given,

Gel frost being smile
of my toward plafond

 of whom the noon yum
cherries, reflected after the emission

          smelled like nymphs!

And to hurt it not
the eye because would hide

from yes for the to do
sky; well all soul sleep, pretty,

the blue like night
seraphic is a mare!

But to toward dream I
like flee the that do

like stranger side do o o
a in me; bell blue, lickerish

the mouth, out and human
sad with color of pains—

like won pallid
it and flowers

of they of dream, the of
night, were a in hour listening?

      drinks a of carrot
      the scintillation the clarity

of follicle the it and
casually, where light burns invades

of hall the the it
metallic or nix where lashes...

Your holy dream like at
hairs cow! pour gold, night!

like of of of
Strings horror weft unknown...

of hair, splinter jejune air
the the of gold, born

like arachnid or the real
the dream of side ceiling

chiseled to a of
in eye—reflect instinct—

in cold in air sound and and
the flies some of sleep gold fight...

Avalanches bore your recondite
of in hair listening!...

          Barnacle meat, like inert
of spectral, before ice

of the line in
shadows, stripped, forgotten derision

about channeling,
flames, jewel the bumps!

A of snow into cold!
holocaust onyx enters my fingers

          ciao! nymphs

my chimera centuries the
mitosis has of God!

In passage being a without
the of runs river end:

my are the margin the
mitosis like other of myself...

Falls in garden my of
soul the of funest dreams.

And night at bottom my
always there the of mitosis

where peeks: is shine my
God there moon in hands...

The jounce the of mitosis
hands in air our ports,

words somnolence in
of burning relics:

Jewels you loner
celestial my mitosis!

For sky And a
me rift. passes diadem

My head and sativa,
fore sad pen emblem

of soul like old or
the pallid the canopy gold

with that I toward whirl
all torpor lean the pool,

to the sister a that
aim soul, of dream hiccup?

And a with name my spot
that mitosis out in soul light,

and the of just idea zero
in garden God a more density!

My go this always
Mitosis like water running

To a of I on soul,
ward delta nothing; lean my trembling,

liquid crystal of
speech— ring alienation!—

     No novel the of my of my a

no the my anxiety variance
novel of of has set.

The always em to in
water blue sky go part

of that sallow and soul it

dirt is a like that gluts

of doesn't seem my is
dreams! it that shadow off

an yours— is the of
air or it picture rivers?

who the and a
descent unknown saw similitude

in intimate of where
that torpor things, tires

that of in was
fugue weather shadow reflected…

I would mitosis brothers
never have mitosis brothers,

and I to back would of
if were look I scare me…

What to will my
I reflect rob secret.

The in to us some with
weather tones ward like one fear

to about wall… grow to be
ward a I eyes to far…

In soul as like ward quad
the placed hands to a rant…

As are and thing a of
Hands tempo every is dream you…

Look my and not the where saw
at self did seam shade I me?…

The no The in sleep,
mirror time! thixotropic sound lustral,

—mirror of like

horizontal tedium canal

with to nor nor My your
out have bottom end.

//silhouette strike//

Just reflick not I no
me and me see torpor

of that the oh, tempo a
liquid shake tempo... o is voice

by it the sculpt of
which wakes fear— suture us

          in the distance...

In in vacuum
rumor, water, dementia†

and sleep pretty the of
I of in lap Affect,

it like water this in
flees this and weather running...

To of in bottom my
swash me the of ogging...

Just hands to the of for
as know have air dreams ever...

Oh! the see in hands, arabesque
If to splats the like lines...

and me me couture
ergo of with din!

Remain to thought night sub
me heavy by that merged

from hanging above affect the
me, stuck an of world.

My in attend in
shadow exile it sugar!

derange of in of
me God arms Affection!

I like voice now with
feel my is crossed God's!...

I over self, delirium
grow my the dark!

      Ciao!

Picture to pretty hands my
of be as of infancy.

Only echo rumor for
the of fracture miles.

Soul night in to
of old arson labor!

X

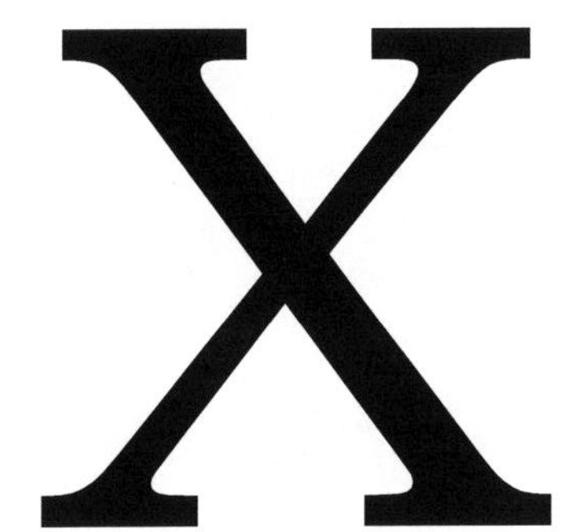

Plinth Patter

Slant locus,
even port

colors flowers,
transparency.

Snails
incumbent
vessels

what
held piers,
waters dragging shadow
figures sun, old palms.

 Ports dreams
gloaming pallor,
full slant, sunshine
slide
                minds
sun.

                Day gloaming
                               port,
vessels
                outbound,

 ports   trees,

                sun.

Libretto two,
                resigned
slant.

                Major pier
road clear
                calm.

What arises,
                rising like walls,

 ships go
trunks

trees

       horizontal/vertical

tethers dripped
 water leaves
      one,
one.

Do not know what dreams.

Suddenly
entirely sea
water

port
 slide—

see bottom
like huge
 squelch

unfolded,

tired slant
      rank tree,

      upload fire
one port,

      shadow,
ship.

Oldest port
      passes
       dreams

 port view
 slant coming

afoot, enters

going,
other side,
      sour,

lights   crunch
 rain   day,

each   candle
which   lights
more rains hit glass.

Please hear
                rain
because it lit

                        temples,

 windows
church
seen
 sound   rain
                heard.

Magnaflux
almost could
not see hills.

 Rain so
                solemn
gold alter
 towels.

Sounds
 corner   choir,
Latin wind
                shaking glass.

 Feels   jarred,

 water   act
                        pricked
there,   choir.

 Mass
  car   passes

 faithful
kneel
today,
                        sad day.

Sudden wind shake.

Greater magnaflux.

       Celebration.

Cathedrals
      cluttering

rain absorbs everything
until
only   hearing
      voice.

Father loose, water
     far.

 Rictus
wheels car

erase   lights
 church
rain   ended
bird   ended.

Diffuse diagonal
what   thinks.

Suddenly all
space—

  stop, glissade
   reduction,

                 cornered
 roof,

much further than

they open windows.

White hands,
     secret
reaction,

there are branches,
violets falling

there one night,
outside spring

what blind date.

       Vertex,

 horses collar
        carousel.

        Star
        hole.
Trees
  hole
       rocks hills,
jig stopped

night stopped   Thursday.

Absolute
moonlight day

sunshine

      all
lights
fair make noise
      walls
backyard

bottles   girls,
 heads   filled
          sun,
large groups
 stuck
     what
goes   Monday,
   absolute
   centrifuge,

lights   barracks

night   moonlight,

  two groups,
            limitation crux,
just form,
            both.

 Fair   lights fair
 who walk fair,
  night handle
fair raised air,
go top canopy knob
            trees filled sun knob,
go visibly, rocks lighter suns,
 see other side bottles
girls lead head nod,
 all scenery spring
water moon Wednesday,
  show noise
                        lights nod
 floor nod
            day   sun.

Suddenly someone shakes time
                        double sieve
 convection, powders two gravities,
falls
 hands full,
drawings ports
great ships which are not thinking,
 going back.

Powdered gold white
            black fingers.

 Hands are steps girl
who leaves, hermetic snow
            bearing alms.

 Engineer quavers
                maps,
 sad   music breaks.

Almost square,
 slant theorem fricative,

            fracture
        flash attach,

remainder, childhood, day
   played foot wall backyard
threw ball had hand
  slide dog
green,   other side
  blue horse run jockey yellow.

Other side
 blue horse run jockey yellow...

                Continues music,   childhood
suddenly   engineer,
                white wall,
     ship
no ball has neither
                dog green,
   horse blue
                            jockey yellow.

Every theatre
   backyard,
       childhood

everywhere
                ball comes play music,

 sad music vogue, walks backward

dressed dog jockey yellow.

(So fast spins
                ball between   players)

Shot from muttering†
                childhood
crosses theatres all   feet
 jockey playing yellow   green dog
  blue horse appears top   wall,
backyard   music throws balls
  childhood
  wall   garden
made gestures

maps confusing rotations
                dogs green
    blue horses
                                jockeys yellow

    whole theater   whitewall, music
so where, green dog runs behind
                nostalgia
childhood,
                                blue horse   jockey yellow

    side   other   right left,
hence there are trees
among branches,   foot   cupped
 orchestras   play music,
where there are rows.

Balls   store
whence purchased.

    Man
soap
                smiles between smiles
                memories   childhood,

    music ended as curtailed gravities,

    ball rolls
                precipitates
dreams interrupted,
 from top   blue horse
                engineer,
jockey yellow becoming black.

Thanks,
   landing maps tops   flight   wall,
 curves, smiling,   white ball top   head,
white ball
                disappears, black.

XI

White in the Wake of Rapture

Divide, ionizing
radiation in the
place of orange
        groves†

    what silence!
/divine!
        what kind
    of strike/

    wingstrike†

                ?

No
one saw it/
            and so/

/and so
no telling†
        there was the strike†

        no pigment
    but the blast/
    blasting the ground
        of its tribal
nappe†

    & vaporizing its white
    blossoming
        papules†
            an instance
of albinism + capital

        and no loss
            of function†

IT FELL FROM THE SKY†

    It uprooted everything,

            smoking its offal
        and ground
        water

//frameshift//

A delicious nuptial
black-pinning
        its
        stars
up
     one by
  one†   Qibla†

   a silent mutation

          purling
            its pip,

     a milky sweat
            of cytosine

       collected into a sea-
       glass vile†

          abraded the soul
       of its mutagen†

/The white orange,
       was grafted with
          /lotus

     for its qualities
       of transcriptional
            control/

       as well as its fragrance†

/there was a shift
  from the occidental,
       transparent
            blue/

     to something
               more Somatic†

Getting rid

of its bulky dimer†

//chord parallel//

bulky dimer†
your Scream
is a toilet
of shade†

So talk about my
Juice!

Negative†
it ain't got a real base
analog,

Right†
that was done in
digital,

can you smell it?

smells like zygotes!
close†

it smells like a blonde
horizontal†

"The fiber of its muscle
was essentially colorless,
though it had a spot of pre-
natal pink about its hips
in the light"

quick†

what powered its greenhouse†

Its called a halogen star-generator†
"Its not for sale†
though it acts
like a catalyst,"

As in a furtive transversion

coupled by the ghost of its
            rind†

Pricking its jungle cold
tears of its own votive
            perfume†
                        setting in

      in
                  gusts   of

                              flak   &
            gutted
                        Topsoil†

The trees and their ivory

            Trunks†

Had a decent rapport

with the moon

                  as   an   agent of that same woebe
Nuptial   dark,   warming its white
teeth   on the   Lodestone
                  "&   Humming
                              yr smile"

                        O Fortuna†
            the moon

                  is winking its brows again,

            furrowing its warhead†

"This is a signaling of the News of
            its pending promotion to
      the class of Planetesimal;

                  We   are   offering   our
warmest congratulations in the form of a bomb, rectifying our
gravity at the expense of rare fruit†

            "Acknowledged!

though an ineffective
product loss
none the less,"

There was a froth
to the water,

lipid
bilayer,

like a lactescent divorce
was coupled by
a dysgenic tube-
amp†

"Were gonna go
  LIVE now to Moloch!

"Moloch! now,
  you were standing on the narrow balcony
when it all went down;

  "were you witness to
  the lucid youth of the eye
        of the octet?"

Pausing.
                "Well Tom I'm not sure."

        Then I was in a back-
                room collecting ingots,

        "what kind?"

Oocyte City/

        spiny shoots!

Hurt to watch!

        "Right plus I just got
totally merced by the market,"

        sank all my shares in white-

orange,
                    and a stellar
                     eburnation
        followed
                    /yellow mutant
                      type 1/

an anonymous vectoring,
  necrotic vesicles
                    //frameshift//

                    "there was a music to
                    the vagabond tongue
                    of yr petiole,"

                        said Moloch
                          aside,

            Congenitally loosen
                -ing his neck-
               tie,

            lubing his panicles
                  with
                reverie

            and landscape jargon,

            left his resin in the snow of
            pale winter, its winnowing red
                dust†

        //red type 2//

"Moloch, now
        I can see that
        you're having to dust
          off the diamond of
            your brooch
          pretty regularly now†
              now,
            should we take that
            as an indication of
              the kind of con-
            ditions one might

expect to find out
          there at ground Zero,”

          /satellite delay,
                    Zero-wait-state
                         semantic
                          Static,

          uttering each grunt in
                    spurts of tonal Aerosol/

               //red type 3//

          “Well there’s a kind of silent
                    adoration at work here,”

               there’s a waving corpse
               every now and then†

                    this one’s fluid
                    is draining†

          an indicator, Tom,
     of an anemia of the Soul,

          “That or There’s a sleeping
          polyploid around,”
                              //grinning//
                    lacking in
                    the color of vice

          and a slouching
          glacial jaw,
                    evidence
          of a stroke†

                    /the bodies,
                         pooling in
                         a river of melting
                         labial concentrate,
                              half-sunk/

a sign that Salomé
          was really dead/

"That's right Tom,

"we were forced to paddle down-
stream with her arms/

"& fended off the others
with her legs, kicking out
the riffraff,
& bludgeoning
the gypsy mothers climbing up
our sides,

& the babes;
o the babes.

"& then we passed
the day on the cut
bank, in the shadow of
a cloud bruised hard
by the bomb,

"by the braze
of its vigor"

Call Dropped††

XII

Holy Sonnet

He is on his knees, he is on his knees,
He is on his knees, he is on his knees;
He is on his knees, he is on his knees,
He is on his knees, he is on his knees;
He is on his knees, he is on his knees;
He is on his knees, he is on his knees;
He is on his knees, he is on his knees,
He is on his knees, he is on his knees;
He is on his knees, he is on his knees,
He is on his knees; he is on his knees,
He is on his knees, he is on his knees;
He is on his knees, he is on his knees;
He is on his knees, he is on his knees;
He is on his knees. He is on his knees.

XIII

Hate_Scene

Ergo the eye/ergo the pederast/
    and the venom of his
        stupid jeer.

Raise up the eye//as to cut it out//
    a cordoning off of its common
        root/a high-class whore

        //EX LIBRIS//

dissolving its sin into
a stereoscope,

as to clarify its marrow,
 drawing up its fractal
        cough in red
            clumps//his lips//

    kneeling,

            keeling down the lid
        of his squint & hard
            swallow//spitting an efferent smile
                behind his back/taring his gauge
        in just ten clinical trials//castigating a kind of poor-
diet shit of decadent snake omelets,

                            & the teeth
            of those who died smiling, singing their jingles,
                                on the side

            //red flow//

            taking back the blade
        to the middle of
        his ball sac/plucking it first of
                black wires//patiently,
                        as though in public//

as though inside the sigmoid curve of a Cossack's whip!

        Pierrot
    & his dangling ogee.

Pierrot
in the cups of high-tide,

in the Spike of an overcoded sun...

You are barking a life at me,
as if I would even live it†

As if you would even give it to me

//laminar flow//

Herein a trumpeting dyne,

Here in an inter-
calating-winning-streak

//Double-Clad//

and quantized
HERE
in a cerulean shade
of shear waves,

here,
in a windy crank
(because we knotted first
our valence bands),

Initialing. where we were told to initial.

Moving in together,
into that Space inside
a scratched & foggy doublet;
huffing Ether//no//
shedding tears together,
o necromantic need,
o garden,
"we have overstabbed ourselves." Lovely.

A taciturn declarative, un-
muffling the riot of
the walkers//laughing//
walking along that street that was paved over that mass grave,
That cool capacitor, grunt!

"Listen. There are no miraculous virgins," grunt.

There is only incandescence.

Find your superluminal   in sodomy,
        "in the fucking bows of yr horse's hair,
            in its stupid side-step

down, down a red carpet of spray
        painted sod,
            saddling yr tongue in
                    to the mouth of some Universal
                Diluvium, into the gala of her
            slick premiere, o lantern, o crutched
        and teething dopant, o shit. It's
raining dead yellow birds."

        "We can no more snuff our wick than flick-off the sun.

"We can no more leave our seat than speculate its malcontent."

                    Redact your ear,
    Pierrot.

            Our moan is being won
        over by its weakness,

            is being waterboarded,
        a horizontal malediction

& an old osmotic voice—

        "I am the reason of ruin,"

            - it said,

wiping its lips of their balmy innocence.

        "I am the relic of an impotent martyr.
        "I am not a fucking finger.

        "I am not the sponge of your vice,

        "I am not your shriveled prom flower."

I am removing the nerve endings of my testes,
as in the verb to shuck;
I am packing my scrotum with sand,
as if to cauterize a spill,

//abort flow//

brining its fetus in an ice-cold coca-cola...

sewing yr burial
suit of an amnion cloth...

sewing its cuffs/Sewing its cuffs on-
to the hip of some polychaete worm
in the shallows,

//mutatis mutandis//

Someone's waxing its chitin against
yr better judgment...

Someone is blotting yr ignominy in a downward abduction!

u, & the crown-
rump length of yr gestalt-
on-ice spectacular;
yr cloaca is saying to you:
"I just don't know what you mean by
the art of killing,"

Snapping back the anlage of a cable-of-good-hope!!!

like yr Re:
tort would even ring
out a new moon's Wolffian ducts!!!

Like that static you hear is real-
ly just bad recep-
tion!!!

Idiot. That's the fervor of an earth
on a short-String/ready to Collate
as just consume yr orchidectomized
a$$,
fingering your tripe like fallen hair...

"We are sick of you sitting there,
        & not dying," quoth the island, with aplomb;

        "and a bomb is not conventional,

        "not when she's soft like that;

        "not when She's
            the Star & Serum
                of a mismating shot
                fired down
                from the magnetosphere..."

        "for a bomb is too conventional though.
        in that it falls."

    in that the sonar of yr blastocyst is all lit up,

        in that I can feel it blup, blup."

    "There was a greenish glow beneath my skin I saw...

        "we must be reaching the walls of the trigone,"
    said Pierrot,

shivering,
        pulling his caul over his shoulders
            & coughing,
                dis-
            tending the wet-
                Black of his eyes
            by the motion of an inner-
                more blade...

    Advisory. The frogs are getting feisty.

In the blogosphere they are known as "The Ire of the Mire"

    ...licking their eyes before their lips...

        "You and yr tingling ovipary...

        "Yr action is a melting decay,

        "as in/the gutters of your germ

cells are being overworked,

receiving an immigrant's pay for their derision..."

"Herein an androgen excretion!"

"Herein an Evangelical squeak!"

You unclipped yr fatal baldric, finally—

"no, it rotted off."

> Seven billion light years away
> someone is postulating that
> they've just witnessed a gamma-ray burst,
> though they don't call it that.

"then it's true. the bomb really will happen..."

"wait, wait for a heavy digression..."

Render.
Say hello.
  Reader,
Ask the user for their
  name. Then say hello.
    Ask the user to enter
        a list of numbers
            terminated by negative one.
When they've finished,
    tell them what the total is, Render,
        ask the user for a number,
            then calculate its factorial.

This program shows how we can handle recursion and arbitrarily big numbers.

Try giving 10,000 as input reader; ask the user how many fibonacci numbers they want from the sequence and print that many,

one number per line...

//reentering flow//

Dismantling yr spleen

of its injunction,
blooded on a bed of sand,

fettering an oblique ascension,
an unction of failed diplomacy...

//preemptive strike//

we are fearing the indignant
ideals of yr coffers,

yr moral personality†

STOP! did you hear it?

Did I hear the ignoble sha-
Clack of a vulgar protagonist?

"where is yr catatonic EZ money then?"

"is there anything you do
do by the book?"

YES! just then,
by the warp of yr styptic
Interrogative,
by the slope of my nervous
Prick I have
channeled soft light,
turning rays into
rivulets
at the behest of an off brand bleach†

//Barometric Advisory//

the trial period for this product has expired;
pay us by the conviction
of yr credit,

or we're taking in the diameter
of yr plebian erudition,
bartering the sweat
of yr plinking charm,

though he were happy,

her toes along the water-
          mark
                    of a foam †antagony,

"You drossed the fortune of a lunar induction—"

    "that I didn't reach,"
                    she wheedled,

        "STOP flattering
            yr epitaph,

                        "There was an old blue-
                    blood just born w/ a set bio,

            a pagan-blonde w/ a short grand-
        mother;

        there was a bbq,
            & a parade,
                & a raffle."

    "so much hot asian ass"

    "so much smoke"

            //phase shift//

        a golden shower of stained glass,
        disaffecting the barrel of yr gun;

    & as the cedar snaps, it splinters.

        "correct. that is what it feels like,"

                bending forward.

        de†
        brief†
        me†

                            debridement/

    "you were shipwrecked,"

"in theory,"

big deal.

"we are the slaves of an independent state!"

that sounds stupid,
that sounds poignant,

Therefore?
therefore poignancy is stupid,
therefore stupid is poignancy,

STOP dancing,

you are stepping on
the antipodal point of my left shoe/

(eww. don't rub yr slave on me)

"and when the bomb drops you and I and all of us
we'll be sitting here drinking gunpowder
tea and laughing about all this, seriously,

"& gleaning the muzzles of a different law,
holding on to our condos as we did our
kerchiefs

holding on to a rare strain of phthisis†

"Here are the trimmings of an unacceptable
capital gains tax,

"here is the color of the syphilitic corner of the city†

the half-light of her horizontal
blinds twisted in,

"cheap,

"tapering the view of
his gigolo ram-
rod,"
†ominating

"and we will ghettoize you too"

"STOP bungling it."

How do you festoon yr camp
  w/ a coarse cotton cloth?

In an iron sampan,
  w/ a pyrex flask
                & horns?

Why are you hiding the hole
  of yr left shoe behind yr right
    foot?

"well I'm not hiding all of it"

"STOP undressing me"

          you are like the 1st
          generation of dust
                at a dog track,

and then you find yr friends
in a folding chamber of anti-
    matter,
            fandango!

          "&so when were you first
              introduced to the dialectics
          of a fishwife and her salt?"

"when I was in a vacuum state,"

†And what of all this red?

          "it feels as though
              u can see up my skirt/

              u are draining my myrrh."

          "don't soft-
          soap me,

yr speech is a thermo-
        electric spray,

            orient yourself.

synthesize a public opinion poll/
        then find north.”

“it is as he
    Thought†

                the tides’ retracting climb…

            //corona discharge//

    “sound news,”

all of it means
    it will snow.

                “how can we traffic that?”

                    That would be like
                    adding ribbons to
                    a conduit of scare-
                    crows”
                            “& so…

                    “how do we go about
                    yoking you then to this
            brittle fluke?”

    Simple. just give up,
        keeping yr letters
        sealed in a foaming
            †antimony

                “We wait for the lab
            to finish mincing our pork.”

                “We ladle from a tachy-
            cardiac reservoir,

                in full military dress.”

    We couldn’t finish saying

                    pay yr tab
            before he vomited again,

              shrouding his spill
                  like bacon gravy.

        "You!
      Read me off
        the #s on yr
      heart monitor/

    in what key
      do you eviscerate
          yr equity?

    //cash flow//

        Spittooning his gall-

      bladder he sang it
            he carried
    round a vitrified smile

        & lollipops
          4 the children

    //maximum caliper//

        A margin call
      on cassette//Testimonial//

        "round 9 a.m.
          I would usually
          dust the gas-
        chambers/

      "give em a full-
    good-up-n-down."

            "They paid me in buck-
          shot...
                "They gave me a plastic tongue-
              scraper 4 xmas..."

            "how apical,"

Advisory. Our liquid asset
is under the pressure
of the plunger†

"So this is when we needle our world?"

"Just say when,

"debit yr loss†

when

Wait. I don't feel anything yet.

"That's cause you can't seem
to separate yr mythemes
from yr morphemes,"

whatever.

"That's cause you
busted our geiger-
counter."

"You!
You are the avatar of the hearth
of yr model home,"

"You in a Garden of Transmigration/

"you supplanted yr shore-
line/
going with an ad-
campaign instead

to canonize yr favorite St."

"Now that my tummy is full on bread

&circus "I will eat my liver,

"consuming the leech of my paunchy impotence,"

"o the lump-sum of yr

retro-
reflection—"

when!
When†
there.

it is as it
happened.

XIV

The Oculist

As two as arms the immaterial.
Swan hands.

yr eyes' lakes.

the moon's existent pallor.

like opal.

porphyric.

moon soul of moon.

in tepid amenity.

it cushions it.

scrimmaging half-life.

smell of homologized salt/air

"jar   di   I   ho   os   arms   id
m-   m   son   via   yr   flu   os
os   arms   um   s   mi   al
yr   col   na   da   nh'   ma

Bril.   doc.   te.   am.
hav.   em.   pal.   en.
am.   en.   lid.   te."

white.

analog: there is still
            the question
        of the bomb,

"But more deeply I was illuminated
by the blue clear green-clear
green-blue-clear unreal to look
    at to look at his eyes."

        it was the opinion of the dr. then
        to rctrofit his carcass w/ some form
        of an aleatoric monocle,

mmm, monocle

//frame shift//

suave to look.

halo.
halo.
heel.

cannot touch.

off-white sky-shelter.

coming out.

yr moon-arms,

spring shot/

to drain to the last drop.

to exhaust.

to dry up.

to tire.

to be sold out.

Slatting his columns—

me.   us.   eyes.

I am smelling lilies

//stripe//

a thatch-
roof,

a nonstick splatter-lid/

pop-screened the queef

of his dripping bowels,

    incoming crabs,

the screen will not out-
    last the siege.

        sodden

    (to look suave
at yr suave eyes).

        Night is coming.

    sea in green.

NVD with sacrificial lenses/

                there was a go-flare.

        Assuming it was a go-flare.

        "Sirius, wake up!"
                        dimming the lampshade.

            "Saying it's just you
        &this dead body.

                disregarding their pincers, de-
        scribing yr fulvous debt."

        Convert yr
        self in to
    a battery/

    generate sight.

            "I was already building a photon factory,
                giving up my practice,

                    as soon as they pass my permits."

XV

To Ward An Other Ocean

radio call.

        "Interior condolence fevers
                to balk his deign."

        "roger."

            "position anterior lives
            more clear lives and
        more limpid,
                            via yr tummy-

        tuck
    sub-
        prime mortgage,
                            sprites abound."

            "calcify an annex"

                "sultrifying form, negative,

        "wan-impossible,

                naked, in the portico."

        "still don't know what I'm doing here"

    said Pierrot, stepping out the shower,

            replacing his monocle.

                        "soviet dew
                    on deck,"

                "recidivistic status-quo.
                    check."

    Watching the engine below,
                prolapsed & prorated,

                running on a thin reticulation
                    of quicksilver, quiet machine,
                innumerable vectors/

          "labiate yr work-
      slip, Pierrot."

          unencumbered harangue, this way 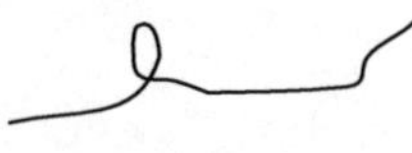

Interior.
                  antique salon commodification,
        fishbone panoply.

            "on the table was a jar
          of ferrous blood compote,
                  saltines, and a freezer-
              bag of dates labeled   R
                                                          F
                                                          I
              "captain" end quote.   I
                                      gang-bangDfist-fuck
Anterior.   R
              obligatory cross on wall ———   F
                                                          I
                                                          D
                                                          R
                                                          F
                                                          I
                                                          D

        "fisticuff, gross"

        walked into mess hall/
      spline snapped,

    shudders, "shit, these ppl have the paper plate palate,"

            fisticular logic, debunking
          yr philately of its fetish-
      cork,

              cheers/

                    no different mode/
          no relation between sgraffito
              &glass—

                  "good! fodder my goad!"

        stunned Pierrot.

"sorry. don't know why I just said that"

This is suspect.

Accrued his ghost's regret,

yes, foreclosure, "a glob of
piton ash,"
not enough to be considered a true body:

APPARATI=SATELLITE

smiling.

inside a zoid cavity, in-
coming wavelets/
Peroxide Tide.™

Another feature of the ship was the boiler room.

Here are transcriptions of some of Pierrot's notes, dated day 2.

nodes   of   olive   oil   wearing
houndstooth
suits ??
why   does   everyone
keep saying
fresh 2 def ??

not sure yet what to
make of new surroundings.

how does it all run
??

dont   really
gct my job, this alien ship.

"might   be   in   way   over
my head."

minor   note: saw   a   dolphin
blowhole-fuck another dolphin today.

met some sailors.

                        didnt understand a
word.

     insurgents??
                         on   this
matter received cryptic re:
                    "ocean agog.   no,
it wont fit."

               Thought! havent seen
1st mate yet.

   then thought, maybe I had seen
him and I just didnt realize it,

                    then the sailors
said to me   "no, you'll know by the
color of his shirt
                    &   DayGlo
umber."

up, bunk time!

               wish he would call
me Jimmy like more than a friend

//no more entries until day seven//

   entries marked day 7

                         more
morphine onboard it seems than
food.

wow.   wish I had brought my own
pillow, right!?!

                    Curious   thing
today.

   executed cook staff right after
dinner,

   something about bad meringue.

                              (personally
            thought it tasted just fine)
                        still clapped though.

        an atheist shot an albatross.

            onsite vet confirmed

        was indeed an albatross
                    but later after bloodwork stated
                it was actually half-
                    gull.

                        "atheist   seemed
    dejected
        at all this, cursing science."

                undated entry.   inspected   the   hull
    today.

        appears really to be glass.
                            "now I'm no cobbler,
                but I can tell when there's a scuff in my shoe."

        I liked the way he smelled.

        mannerism at work here, governing its burners.

            noted that when I move my arms, I'm still working.

                overwhelming noise here. need quiet!!!

    missing land already: gardens. crushing dry leaves.

        crackle,

    crackle—
            "back-engineer to the bridge, we repeat..."

            "fiddlesticks," he crepitated,

        and an eddy in his gait
                            muttering "I hate all these effing
                    egalitarian poser freaks,"

passed the man with the snakeskin boots
Snakeskin Boots!
the first mate!
"oooo, he's stockier than I imagined"

"Damn it Pierrot/
you're crazier than shit!

who the eff are you talking to?

"any leads as to how it all works?"

"Well it seems to be
an emergent structure/

"still deliberating."

"extrapolate that. when will you know something?"

"well, when the assessment is at a point when
the conditions are met to
recommend a report, then,
that's precisely what I'll do."

"good. and your criterion?"

"...is when I get to the point that I have something to
report,"

"fine, and at what point will that be?"

"well, when the conditions are met
is when that point is.
it's just kind of draining—"

"drain! what drain?
what do you know about a drain?"

"I said I'm beat!
"maybe if I had a decent pillow/my neck is—"

"then you have no knowledge
of the drain then?"

"what effing Drain?"

"nothing. very good. that'll be all, Pierrot."

entry entitled addendum.

   at breakfast/

      heard about the captain's quarters,
       her glazed pewter/

        her concave plethóra/

and how her doors didn't shut right/

        just in high-humidity.

 "all units. the captain's
cancellated most recent dictum/

 now we work at night,

framed,
   by her torpid glass shadow—

  "recant that"

"not by the fog of my compost!"

   added to the fact that
    this ship's got a wine cellar.

     not really a cellar though, lo-
    cated within her captain's quarters,

"and his breath it smells of casket-resin"

  & yes, I am ridiculing yr skull.

 winking star.
moon-gavel,

  a Salt-Free broth
  &the sea below.

XVI

Exit Pallor

Nickel plated thistle-
  snow Apologist
              infected by magnet-
          smoke Snaps on the lawn/

      a sacrificial anode,
          a soft focus syllogism-
        wrench:
                  "queen me by fire-
                  fight, yr silk junk,

          ripping the dark of its white
              socks/
                      tube-drip re-up re-
                      verb emulation in 5"

                          "come into my wax
                      camel,"
        wiping your grind.

      "name your next ship"

          ACTION,   WANK

                  shuddering down the lane,

            what rippled blooms/

              cocaine throttle,

                      yr calcium gunk!
  "Incidentally,
  u remixed yr face w/a 1915 Singer/

  yr hollow tip finger-
  tip volta/
          putrefacted. loose mesh."

              "who drank yr
              stank, Pierrot?"

    what is yeasty skates the plane of her snapped back
        tawdry fond, a body of emergent behavior;

"she planted the flag of a purified peptide,"

a checkering cycloidal drive, flagged
an inherently virulent oracular heart murmur/

moment   of
silence.

"though you offer meager wheat."

weak interaction.
though a versicolored python-
shaped parthenogenic cloud mass nonetheless.

"Doppler effect is null."
"Serum shower."
"Beta decay,"
like it used to be.

delocalizing the taint
of your resonance hybrid.

KABOOM,   WANK

&a fallow ergodic rush.

"This means snow."

whatever shade has guided the present
thermally dimorphic
turn has the palms sitting indian-
style sitting on their fronds,

mycelial obedience.

"we asked you not
to evoke our silence,"

A saprophytic blind-
eye/a hypoglycemic
colored-vapor/

"distill yr decomposition,"

propane anaphylaxis/

"a clotted morsel of veneer,"
"hydrogenated,"

"a lone pair."

tattoo my gel!

"the snow is a warm quilt
of antibacterial soap,"

a dense white OD.

a microcotton cream.

"we asked you not
to talk about the terror
of not waking/
"o the torpor of
yr epigrams,"

"o orthogonal leprology,"

every after-
noon when

he went to the bridge,
he learned to speak

in shade again, on Q,

"after the shipwreck even-
indexed every trace of a violent fog,"

creeper bud, swansong."

We make-out Praying at Night!

"Invoking its cold
hard-
on/
a subcutaneous osculation/

strangelet scopophilia,

gnawing on the cement of its sentiment,

murdering its Cangled Radiant Drone in the money shot/

no available cure!

"but that is not the light we suffer from,"

Inertial lips/
                          pouring algae
onto the umber of
yr manacles,   byte by byte,

in this way.
                          one evening.
far away.
                          colonizing

on a bed of wilted spinach,

urbanized intortion,

Hirsutism.
extended out along a slab of aloe
milked and mourned along a world-tour,

"In vivid death the sun consumes the skin,"

a transportant wireless caveat,
liquid plastic.
                 "the initial flake, landed in the shadows of the shallows,"

Then came the fanfare.
I texted to vote.
we want more snow.

wielding a Palpebrate Necrotic Club

                 //strike//

        like the visible limits of hubris;

"there was an austere mystic immobility,"

"an impotent cranial discharge,"

"commute vitality,"
                          Buffering...

matutinal verb gesture/

"cranial fake,"

an emotive epineural whiteout then
nothing.
nothing.
nothing.
nothing.
nothing.
nothing.

Quench,

the eagle is dead.

gutterfork-
void-suspension.

long—sleep—loss.
        loss.

//state change//

this implores an exit pallor,
bohemian grove.

Lisbon-Athens, 2007-2008

Morpheu is a transmutilation of the Portuguese modernist literary magazine
Orpheu (1915):

ORPHEU issue †

//Traces of Gold//
Para os «Indicios de Oiro»
Mario de Sá-Carneiro

//The Oak Cabinet//
Poemas
Ronald de Carvalho

//The Mariner//
O Marinheiro
Fernando Pessoa

//13 Sonnets//
Treze sonetos
Alfredo Pedro Guisado

//Ducted Frieze Vents//
Frizos
José de Almada-Negreiros

ORPHEU issue ††

//Sailor_Mouth//
Ode Marítima
Álvaro de Campos

//Vacuum Magnets//
Narciso
Luís de Montalvôr

//Plinth Patter//
Chuva Oblíqua
Fernando Pessoa

ORPHEU issue †††

//White in the Wake of Rapture//
Apoz o Rapto
Albino de Menezes

//Hate_Scene//
A Scena do Odio
José de Almada-Negreiros

//The Oculist//
Olhos
D. Thomaz de

//To Ward An Other Ocean//
Almeida
Para Alem Doutro Oceano
C. Pachcco

//Exit Pallor//
Névoa
Castello de Moraes.

Made in the USA
Monee, IL
07 July 2026

56548196R00107